SECRET WARRIOR

"My process-driven coaching is firmly grounded in relationships and support for mental health. In sports, this includes both the coaches and the team. Coach P has beautifully captured the essence of this balance in *Secret Warrior*."

—Nick Saban
Head Coach, University of Alabama

"In *Secret Warrior*, Coach P is vulnerable and transparent. She shares personal coaching stories throughout a very successful head-coaching career regarding mental wellness, personal growth, team loyalty, and thriving with her teams through adversity. Her authenticity shines through in *Secret Warrior*—a compelling memoir that travels well beyond the court."

—Mike Krzyzewski
Head Coach, Duke University

"In *Secret Warrior*, Coach P shares in-depth stories of mental health resilience and perseverance where the team and coach come together to thrive. Such a story demonstrates the need to keep the conversation going . . . and truly realize how mental health matters."

—Tara Vanderveer
Head Coach, Stanford University

"Successful coaching involves a great understanding of people, and the stories behind the student-athletes and coaches. The off-court understanding and development, for both the players and the coaches, is critical. In *Secret Warrior* Coach P brings to life a story that includes such relationships, and the willingness to fight back under unique circumstances."

—Tom Izzo
Head Coach, Michigan State University

"Impaired mental health has no boundaries as all races, ethnicities, and families worldwide are affected in so many ways. In Coach P's *Secret Warrior*, she explores an authentic story of struggles and triumph within sports. However, the lessons are profound and can apply to us all."

—C. Vivian Stringer
Head Coach, Rutgers University

"I have known Coach P for thirty years. She is truly an inspiration. Regardless of how tough life gets, she continues to be a warrior. Her book *Secret Warrior* is going to help many and move mountains relative to understanding and thriving with mental and physical health. This book reminds us all to keep faith in the journey . . . and to share our stories courageously. "

—Ruthie Bolton
Olympic Gold Medalist, WNBA Champion, Motivational/Faith Speaker

"CoachP reminds us all that, at any moment life can take an unexpected turn. She allows us into her quiet moments with God. God was winking at her in preparation with what was to come. Faith, family and friends guided her to give the readers an incredible story of hope and strength."

—LaChina Robinson
ESPN Analyst

"There is no doubt Coach P and I share a love of basketball and great experiences at Duke as well. But, most importantly, we both love people and relationships. In *Secret Warrior*, Coach P shares an incredible personal story that compels the reader to see the big picture relative to mental health in such an authentic space as sports. Mental health impacts everyone worldwide. A must-read memoir, Coach P may have coached her best championship game in sharing this story."

—Reggie Love
Senior Advisor at Apollo Global Management, Vice President and Head of External Affairs for HRS Management; Reggie also served as the personal aide to President Barack Obama from 2009 to 2011

"My teammate, CoachP, strikes a chord with the focus needed to share stories and create real change in mental health nation and worldwide. Her story is compelling and authentic while addressing the mental health stigmas affecting people of every background, ethnicity, and age group. A timely share, and a must read for all."

—Anucha Browne
UNICEF USA, Chief Engagement, Advocacy, and Global Programs Officer

"With courage and authenticity CoachP takes us behind the curtain and brings awareness to the importance of relationships and mental health. A powerful memoir and a must read by anyone who believes relationships are integral to our human experience."

—Molly Fletcher
Former Sports Agent, Author/Speaker

Secret Warrior

A Coach and Fighter, On and Off the Court

By Joanne P. McCallie

Published by

◤ köehlerbooks™

3705 Shore Drive
Virginia Beach, VA 23455
800–435–4811
www.koehlerbooks.com

SECRET
WARRIOR

A Coach & Fighter, On and Off the Court

Joanne P. McCallie

VIRGINIA BEACH
CAPE CHARLES

To my British mum, Christina Clark, for your incredible strength, leadership and love. To my father, Captain Robert Palombo, for your ever-lasting humor and love, who left us suddenly during the writing of this book.

And to my loyal husband, John, and our thoughtful children, Maddie and Jack: thank you for your support, loving spirit, courage, and sense of life in all that you bring to our special family.

CONTENTS

TIPOFF

I have always wondered when would be the right time to share the story of my affliction with bipolar disorder in a way that I could motivate, inspire, and also raise awareness—and truth— about mental illness and all the attached stigmas that come with the imbalanced brain. I have chosen this moment to reflect and reveal my private battle with mental illness to show that those afflicted can be successful, productive, and happy.

I am a wife, mother of two, and until recently, was a competitive and successful Division I head basketball coach: for thirteen years I led the Duke University women's team. Before that, I was head coach of the women's teams at the University of Maine, my home state, and at Michigan State University. I was raised in Maine in a small town, and was always competitive as a kid. I parlayed my skills as a high school basketball player into an athletic scholarship at Northwestern University in Evanston, IL. From there, I went on to coach at Auburn University as an assistant coach, then on to Maine, Michigan State, and finally Duke as head coach.

Of my twenty-eight years as a head coach, twenty-five have been as a person diagnosed with bipolar I/II disorder. Despite my mental health disease I have persevered, but not without struggle: I have sacrificed and marshaled unrelenting determination, and I have tried to instill those traits in my talented basketball players, my own kids, and countless others who know me or of me.

My brain chose its own path when I was thirty years old. I was a young mother, a wife, and a new basketball coach ready to take on the demands of Division I women's basketball. Like many who go through struggles with brain imbalance, I found it hard to sort the proper cause, catalyst, and then, of course, the treatment. For many, it is a lifelong journey of learning, growing, grieving, accepting, and then flourishing with a newfound balance within your own brain. For me it was so.

I had experienced natural childbirth approximately one year prior to my first manic-depressive episode. With a new and stressful job, and a new baby girl, my life was full and challenging. Perhaps the situation was ripe for a mental collapse. It is tricky to sort through the numerous details of the events prior to my first episode. Timing and causation blurred. Sometimes you never truly know the full story of why things happen. Looking back for answers can torment. It can delay acceptance of the new reality.

That "not knowing" has caused me shame and fear for much of my life. Sharing the details and diagnosis with family members alone can be daunting: sharing with friends, professional associates, and strangers is even more so.

For instance, I recall a family dinner at my parents' house that was eerily quiet and uncomfortable. I had just started my meds and my mind was not quite right yet. As we sat down to enjoy yet another great home-cooked meal by Mom, there was quiet banter of no real significance. No one truly knew what to say or ask. After a few uncomfortable minutes of silence, my mom asked, "What is this all about? Where did this come from?"

She was voicing her well-meaning and authentic thoughts about the elephant in the room, but they were overwhelming to me at that moment. I felt my stomach clench with anxiety. There was a complete unease about my presence. I wanted to escape. Why was I suddenly so different? What was wrong with me? Would this anxious state continue? I had no answers that evening. I just responded, "I really don't want to talk about it right now."

The truth is, I really could not talk about it then. I just wanted to leave, to hide behind a wall of silence. I left my parents' home with no answers given. Space, and breathing slowly, were my answers as I departed. I wanted to turn away from my loved ones. There was too much fear in their eyes. Everyone was so uncomfortable and lacking in knowledge of the science, and in my recovery plan. I was much more comfortable with the doctors seeking answers, away from family. I wanted no pity or ignorance, intended or not. At that time, all my energy had to be directed inward. Much later in my healing, a dear therapist always ended our sessions with, "be good to you." It was to be a long process to understand the true meaning of those four words.

———

My battle with mental illness, an affliction faced everyday by countless adolescents and adults in this country, continues. Approximately nine million Americans are affected by the long continuum of mental health impairment in the form of the bipolar disorder, the disease I have suffered with. It is an equal-opportunity affliction that does not discriminate by economic class, race, gender, or age. It is a powerful human condition with which the victim must cope and endure, fighting a battle that can last a lifetime. So, by bringing my personal battle out of the shadows, and into the broader light of life challenges, I hope to educate, enlighten, and give a voice to the secret warrior in all of us.

Mental illness is, first and foremost, a disease, a sickness like so many others that can impair people worldwide with crippling symptoms. It's an illness that can disrupt daily life and strain even the most solid marriages or relationships. Too often, partnerships cannot endure all the trials. Fight or flight comes into play with both the diagnosed and the partner. The individual with the unquiet mind is most at risk. The upheavals are real. Fear drives distrust and irrational thinking. A beautiful mind can turn upside down, drive people away, and hurt those whom they love. That's precisely what transpired with me while I was coaching at Maine.

Like many former athletes, I generally refused to accept the idea that my body would fail if I was not in control. My mind eluding me at the pinnacle of my career was unfathomable. The realization that your mind and brain balance can just completely take over your will, without warning, and with such scary consequences, is life-changing. There is perpetual fear of the unknown. A haunting reality invades your space, your life, and all who count on you. The deep pit in your stomach aches all the time. Your confidence is undercut in the most immediate fashion. Things you always found so natural are now so challenging. In a way, you become mechanical.

Overthinking, and intimidation by your own thoughts, provides a steady stream of doubt. When an athlete loses their natural rhythm in sports, and they begin to overthink their execution, their performance suffers and can be characterized as a form of choking, that mechanical hesitant state of losing faith and fluidity in training. I lost this very faith and fluidity with my life and thinking as my mental illness took root.

———————————

Among the many lessons I have learned over my decades-long fight with the disease is that having a supportive partner, be it by blood, marriage, or friendship, is critical to coping with the bipolar disorder. Soothing words of reason are so critical: they help combat the destructive thinking that lurks when the mind decides to operate on its own terms.

Over the years, I had filled that void for others who suffered as I did, particularly young people who may not have had a partner to play a pivotal role of support. An especially important part of the healing is for the sick person to understand they are not alone, and I have benefited from an incredible person and partner of twenty-nine years, my husband John. Trained as an economist with a chemistry background, a passion for science, and a desire for reason over emotion during critical thinking, John's sound presence provided a healthy human antidote to the shifty nature of my mind. His dedication and keen sense of curiosity and care, has been true love, indeed. The deepest kind.

John's thoughts and memories have been poignant. He has helped me recount and add perspective to my personal journey of great successes and great setbacks. Our life as a couple started in almost storybook fashion. Shortly after being married, we both landed dream jobs at the University of Maine, he as a professor and me as a head coach of the women's basketball team. All was good in our lives, which would soon include wonderful children. But I was a speeding train about to go off the tracks and destroy myself, my family, my career, my team. I didn't see that self-destruction coming, but John did. Signals that something was seriously wrong with me became more episodic, first emerging in subtle ways and then becoming more regular. In writing this memoir, I have leaned heavily on John's recollection of events.

John recalled, "My first real memory is our golf game that one afternoon in the fall with (long-time friends) Terry and Stan. You were very irritable. More than just a bad mood . . . we found it disturbing. We played along as you separated yourself, and played behind us. At that time, we just shrugged it off as stress, or too much on your mind. Then, as we went to the club to eat, I remember you talking to two fans who seemed to know their basketball. They challenged you, and the upcoming team, with a know-it-all tone.

"You just ripped into them, supporting your team and questioning their knowledge. I thought it refreshing to hear you represent your team so aggressively, but then, after the exchanges continued, all I could think about was that this did not sound good. Something is wrong with Joanne."

My affliction seemed to worsen as I struggled to juggle work and family life. There were high expectations for the team, and I was determined to meet them, working countless hours recruiting players, running practices, working on winning strategies: building a program. Being the head coach of a Division I basketball program is demanding: it's a lifestyle, not merely a job, leaving little room for much else. It was during my time juggling expectations and pressures at the University of Maine that my mental disorder mushroomed. I had become manic.

Mania promotes the notion of quick thinking. It also assumes that the random grace notes in life arrive by design rather than serendipity. We all tend to smile and feel good when happy coincidences occur, but are they real? Even after my recovery and years of success as a diagnosed mood-disorder person, such questions can still come to me. Are my feelings of success and good fortune a sign of mania, or an incredible blessing or a timely grace note, or just coincidence? Am I sleeping okay? Is my speech steady and strong? Am I responding to this truly incredible time, or is my mind cycling beyond my control?

Faith over fear remains a constant theme of life. As mood-disorder person, I have been trained to check myself under these more frantic times. But often, a sufferer does not see what other people can see. There is such incredible value of an educated spouse or partner. Their perspective is the key to restoring balance. Otherwise, trauma holds on, baiting anxiety and fear. It inserts itself into your soul. It can rob you of enjoying some of the greatest times in your life.

For me, finding that balance over the past twenty-five years has been made possible by being surrounded by those who care, who have shown great support and competence, and who do not quit. The brilliant mind has tentacles that reach far and wide, it draws everyone to experience the amazing capacities as well as the destructive realities that the altered mind can offer.

———

When the episodes occur with bipolar disorder, it is best to initially seek out only those familiar with the disease to create space for the individual to cope and sort through the myriad of complex emotional issues. The afflicted need to build up some emotional stamina, just as a runner increases mileage to train for the ultimate race. For me, mood disorder was a race in many ways, a marathon much more than a sprint. For me, every day centered on how I was feeling.

I had to train myself to examine my brain daily. I struggled early with all the mental assessments and the constant feelings of anxiety and inadequacy. Would I ever "be me" again? I just wanted to be healthy for my family, my team and staff. I grew tired of this "new normal." The constant self-evaluations were tedious, and were daily reminders that I was now simply different. I truly felt like a formerly normal person turned professional narcissist. There were days and nights of thinking only about myself. For a new mom trying to raise a family, it was not the most comfortable or productive feeling. It was ill-timed and all-consuming. I simply did not have time for this halting path through life. Ironically, and despite the difficulties of the schedule with parenting and the team, those busy times kept me focused on each single task to be accomplished singly. My brain needed balance, but I found I could lock in and be very productive.

Years ago, and still today, there remains a taboo, a lack of understanding surrounding these types of diseases. The subject is hard to talk about with anyone. For years it stayed buried and hidden deep within me, even though I was determined to deal with it and move on as quickly as possible. I was the only member of my family to have such a condition—a psychological outlier. I was out there in a space that no one could conceptualize. Few, if any, felt comfortable asking me anything about my experience. I had an initial great distrust of many around me, a sense of protective paranoia. I did not even trust my first doctor or the medicines she had prescribed.

It was the support of my husband, family, team members, friends, fans that helped get this manic, paranoid train back on the tracks again.

This is my story as I remember it, told only with the hope that my journey will help inform and ease others afflicted, or the loved ones surrounding them. It's a warning, as well, to those who dismiss mental illness as something less "real" than a physical disease. Trust me, it is not less real. Bipolar disorder and other mental illness are chemical, and as with so many other diseases, they do not discriminate by profession, gender, age, race, income, age or location. I hope you find my story a cautionary tale, but also one that inspires and leaves you with hope.

PART ONE

BECOMING COACH P

Growing up in Maine is the greatest gift my parents could ever have given me. The seasons there have a way of bringing in new energy all year. Of course, the summers are filled with the smells of clean ocean air, lobstering, and boating. In the fall, in our small town of Brunswick, we had Halloween parades and outdoor ice skating at the local mall. We had several hot dog stands, and two competed all year—Danny's, a local favorite, and Down East hot dogs. Dad always made sure we gave our business to both, but he had a soft spot for Danny's because the namesake was there daily, talking with customers.

The junior high and high school sports were very well supported. Folks had pride in the Brunswick Dragons. Morse High School's team, the Shipbuilders, were our rival, fifteen minutes down the road. The girls' basketball team at Brunswick High School often outdrew the guys' games in fan support with great pride. Life was filled with apple picking, skiing, and all sorts of outdoor activities.

My parents made huge sacrifices to keep the family in Maine. My father was a Navy pilot. We first were stationed in Brunswick. But later, Dad was transferred to Jacksonville, Florida. My older brother, younger sister, and I were headed for a new life. We tried living in Orange Park, Florida for a year. After my brother Rich was frisked at the high school, and I was caught with a friend smoking in the girl's bathroom, my mom called it quits for Florida. We returned to Maine and happily grew up in small-town America. Of course, my dad had to commute from Florida each weekend to have time at home with us. It was not a perfect way of life, but it worked for the good of the whole. Mom was steadfast about raising her brood in Maine, and there was no going back.

Basketball was a way of life for our family. Early on, it was a plan of mine to seek out a scholarship to play hoops in college. There were thousands of trips to the gym, many games and state title runs, too. I was a five-foot-nine shooting guard who also loved leading from the point guard position. During my four years at Brunswick High, my team enjoyed great support from the community by winning our conference and playing for a state title every year. We began a *gender equity* push for all the women's basketball programs in the area by outdrawing the men's games every season.

I played with a fearless emotion that even led me to hyperventilating when I was younger, in seventh and eighth grade. I had a marvelous coach, the late Allen Graffam, who tried to channel my competitive drive and to develop my game further. We called our beloved high school Coach Koerber "Coach K." I was always in the gym and stayed after school to shoot and work on my game. Coach K let me and my father into the gym on weekends, even though it was not supported by the school rules.

My brother often teased me because I studied hard and then went to bed by nine each night. I was always aware of needing sleep: I just felt so much better with eight hours or more. And I felt that my athletic success during my high school years was because of my committed routine. To this day, I also feel that playing three sports kept me healthy, and by using different muscle groups, I had balanced strengths. I played soccer in the fall, basketball in the winter, and softball in the spring while trying my hand at track, too. Eventually I specialized more with basketball, but always played softball because the coach recruited me hard, saying I needed a break from all that basketball.

I really respected our softball coach, Coach Cockburn, and

happily played second base. He thought I was very quick and could keep the ball in front of me, but my arm and throwing ability was suspect. I always saw myself as a shortstop, a coveted position for fierce competitors, but it became clear that second base was my place. Being selected to the All-Conference team my senior year was pretty cool. Coach Cockburn was right: softball was a good "release" sport from my ultimate passion.

During my freshman and sophomore years during basketball season, I sometimes cried with frustration when we lost. We did not lose often, however. As a junior and senior, I learned how to channel my emotions and share them more productively with the team. I was a captain for both those seasons, and as a senior was voted nationally to the *Parade* All-American Team. This was the most prestigious honor for high school female ball players at the time partly because *Parade* only picked the top forty players in the country. I was upset be to picked fortieth, and to have my name spelled wrong on their publication, but inwardly I was very proud to be named in that great group of players. (I mostly kept my sense of humor about the spelling error.)

Ironically, our state paper had voted me *second best* female high school player in Maine. I wondered how I could be recognized nationally and not be voted the best player in the state? This was my first real feel for *politics* in the sports world. When I first heard this news, I ran to my room and angrily cried in my pillow. The newspaper was a northern publication and the top select was from that region, while I lived in southern Maine. But my mom tried to put it all in perspective as she said, "Don't worry, dear. The cream always rises to the top."

―――――――――――

I enjoyed being a student and an athlete in school. The athletic side of things gave me great confidence. I was able to funnel that strength back to the classroom. I was bright and interested in many subjects, but the on-court success was the underpinning of my success in class: the courses were taught enthusiastically, and the teachers demanded full attention. There were no cell phones, and almost no computer work.

One day stands out, as I reflect upon those years. I was an impressionable high school junior, enjoying a public speaking course at Brunswick High. I enjoyed my classes very much. But, like many, I struggled with nerves when standing in front of the class. Public speaking was a required as we were preparing to be college-bound seniors, and we spoke on many different topics. Occasionally there was an improv day where we did not prepare our remarks but instead simply had to answer questions picked out of a hat: each student would prepare some thoughts on the spot, while the other students listened and evaluated the strength of the answer and presenter's style.

On that day, an interesting question was picked: *What body part can you not live without?* This thought-provoking question was one that everyone seemed eager to discuss. I listened to my classmates— many decided to take a very physical view with their answers. They talked about life without arms, legs, eyes and ears and all sorts of other internal and external parts. When my turn came, my thoughts were precise and unhesitating. I said that I could not live without my mind. It was not about the brain alone, but also about the mind operating, learning, and directing my thinking. I felt a sense of independence and pride in my answer. There was no right answer, of course. But the apparent uniqueness of my answer, indicated by the teacher to me directly, was appreciated. I felt clever. Praise goes a long way in encouraging young minds to push boundaries. And the positive feedback from the teacher locked it into my happy memory forever.

———————

My high school successes earned me an athletic scholarship to Northwestern University in Evanston, IL.

Eventually I boiled down my list of college possibilities to two schools: Duke in Durham, North Carolina and Northwestern in

Evanston. Ultimately, my mom was a huge influence on my choice. My dad was often deployed and was unable to be a part of the decision-making process. Mom allowed me to go to Duke alone for a visit, although she was not keen on her daughter going South to a conference that was still growing. She pointed out that she wanted more sophistication for her daughter. My mom did not get to go to university in England where she grew up, and she was bound and determined her daughter would attend a top private and academically high ranking university.

Mom accompanied me on my trip to Northwestern. We had a great visit and she was captivated by the school on Lake Michigan, and the great city of Chicago. There, Mom saw the sophistication she had wanted for me, and I liked the team dynamic. At that time, the Big Ten conference supported women more than the emerging Atlantic Coast Conference, Mom argued. That sealed the deal.

Despite having chosen Northwestern, I never lost my love for Duke. Little did I know that I would one day arrive there as a head coach.

———————

I first declared myself a radio, tv, film major at Northwestern, but I graduated with a degree in political science. Then one summer, I worked in a law firm in downtown Chicago, thinking I might go to law school. After my summer internship there, I found out first-hand about the excruciating hours in quiet research rooms. The long hours researching legal precedents was too isolating for me.

So after graduation, I worked in sales and communications for a Chicago telecommunications firm. I was completely new to this field, and the only thing that truly motivated me was competing with my co-workers on the quota board, while being able to essentially create my own schedule. I was a major account manager who sold telecommunication service to all folks, business and personal. The cold calls were brutal. I experienced rejection after rejection, until connecting with that one person who was the decision-maker about their firm's telecommunication needs. All-Net Communications was the fourth largest carrier behind AT&T, MCI and Sprint. All-Net were the underdogs trying to expand our clientele and compete with the Big Three. I loved the competition. I began at the bottom of the board. It gave me great pride to work my way to the top spot. It was a feverish nine months. I worked long hours and long days.

I commuted into the city via my old cranberry Volvo. I used the back roads, driving every day through a tough neighborhood called Cabrini Green. I was often naïve, being a small-town Maine girl. I stayed very focused at my work. Commuting efficiently to get to work early, regardless of any dangers, seemed like the thing to do. I lasted less than a year as a sales manager, despite that great feeling of succeeding in a career job right out of college.

I was successful, but unfulfilled.

———————

The former athlete in me was craving to get back to sports somehow, some way. I began my search at various schools for graduate assistantships. My only requirement was that the school was in a state with warm weather, as I had spent five years in the Chicago area, and was ready to warm my bones. I interviewed over the phone with Vanderbilt University. I really liked the coach. Coach Lee said that "Vandy" was the better school in which to pursue a graduate degree. However, I was looking for the best combination of academics with a school that had Final Four experience. I had never come close to going to a Final Four at Northwestern, and I always wondered what it would be like.

I chose to pay my own way to Tacoma, Washington to meet with Coach Joe Ciampi, the head coach of Auburn University. That school was playing in the 1987 Final Four in Tacoma, and Coach Ciampi invited me to meet with the team for the team dinner the night before the national championship. I was so nervous! I arrived early, met one of the vice presidents of the school, and was in awe. Beyond that, the team's dynamic and personality was fun and welcoming, so the choice was an easy one. I committed to be the graduate assistant at Auburn University in Alabama. A new life.

I studied for my MBA while learning how to coach. I even shared an office with Coach Ciampi. It was direct, interesting, and intimate work right from the start. The interesting part of my decision was that my parents were split on where I should go for graduate school. My mom reinforced the academic side, and Vanderbilt was her clear choice. I remember my father asking me specifically on the phone what my objectives were.

"What do you want to do with your future, Jo?"

I replied that I wanted to get an MBA and find out what "big time" athletics is all about.

"Well, then, the choice is easy. Auburn seems to fit exactly what you need."

I could almost hear my mom sigh deeply in the background and say, "No, Robert." But, with my dad's blessing, and despite my mom's trepidation with the "deep South," I was on my way. That bit of advice from my dad changed the trajectory of my life forever.

———————

Excited for my new job and life, I left Chicago in that old cranberry Volvo, alone. For a New England girl, it was going to be another big transition. While in Chicago, I had become a city gal, with city clothes, accustomed to city life. I was swapping the glamour and sophistication for sweats, humidity, humility, twelve-hour days, a new roommate, no friends, but a great opportunity to learn from and work with tremendous student-athletes while being a new, and very small, part of an established Final Four program.

When viewed through the lens of my practical New England upbringing, my career path seemed to meander and made no sense. I struggled mightily the first year at Auburn. Being alone in the South, without family support or friends, was a big adjustment. From the humid weather, to the deep southern accents, to the loneliness and being brand-new with the program, and being in a place where I knew no one—it was an eye-opening experience. I marched on with work, diving into my work in school and with the team. My day started at eight a.m. with classes. Then, it was basketball until about six, then studying until eleven, then bed. The next day I would do it again. At lunch I tried to keep up with Coach Ciampi, running five miles in the scorching heat of Auburn, Alabama.

Southern life and cuisine and the warm folks of Auburn grew on me daily. I was learning from Coach Ciampi, and experienced two national championship games with Auburn. The two most important lessons I learned from Coach Ciampi were to 1) work by objectives 24/7, and to 2) coach my personality every day. Coach came from West Point Military Academy where he had led the women's team, while an up-and-comer named Mike Krzyzewski led the men's program. Coach Ciampi did not mince words, and gave me a strong sense of commitment to achieve at the highest level of the game. He was a military man and thinker. As a Navy brat, I loved it.

━━━━━━━━

I loved getting my MBA, too. My classmates were smart and fun. I had found great friends outside of the team and basketball environment.

At first, I was not sure about coaching as a career. The first year, everything and everyone seemed so intimidating. Learning all the players and their personalities, and having them accept the graduate assistant girl from Maine, was a challenge. It took a lot of work to garner trust and respect from the team and staff because I knew extraordinarily little about coaching at that time. Understanding how to run a program and cover all the details appeared to be an enormous and impossible job. So much work. So much to learn. Coaching, I would learn, is not a job, but a way of life. We worked by objectives 24/7.

By my second year, I was hooked. The kids started calling me Coach P and it stuck. Two point guards helped me realize that coaching was my calling. Chantel was a tricky, talented point guard who daily challenged me as a coach. She had a broad grin to go with a great personality, and oftentimes had a lot to say, but her passion for the game always shined, despite challenges. She led us to great success, and was very talented off the court as well. Her personality and creative mind and love of the program made her a great promoter of the women's game.

Ruthie was so strong-minded that when she wanted to make a point—and have a little fun—she'd pick me up and twirl me around until I got dizzy. I always laughed eagerly as she put me down and watched me stumble.

Ruthie's passion for the game, love of life—not to mention her incredible singing voice and overall leadership—made me want to coach her hard, and learn from her as much as possible. Ruthie expected to be pushed every day, was always listening and never took any comments personally. She had a burning desire to be a champion, and she loved people for who they were, every day. Ruthie led the team to Final Fours and became a gold medalist in the Olympics.

Working with Chantel and Ruthie taught me so much. They gave me purpose within the program, and an understanding of the relationships in coaching. They both were Final Four-point guards who were eager to learn, and wanted to give the Maine girl a chance. I was new and unsure at times, but knew the point guard position relative to skillset, but more importantly for leadership. My enthusiasm as a new coach went a long way in building referent power with the point guards and the team. I always was a quick learner and was not afraid to be wrong. I had no vast coaching experience, and certainly no Final Four experience . . . yet. I listened carefully and began to understand the intricacies of running an elite program. I was hooked.

I had a clear direction after my Auburn experience. I chose a career filled with developing people. I had also chosen a career that is almost bipolar by nature. Coaching the ups and downs of immediate demands for success, while balancing the issues of student-athletes, is a perfect recipe for mania and depression.

The elation of winning and finding success as a team is a wonderful feeling: the highs are very high and the lows are very low. Coaches generally remember the tough losses more than the great wins. We tried to treat each game the same, and pushed to learn more and get better—win or lose. But to any coach and committed team, the losses are brutal. The coach and the great players take the losses very personally. When we win, it is everyone who contributes on the court or the bench. If we lose, it is time for each person to hold herself accountable, with the coaches, of course. Up and down we go through a tough and long season. Of course, the teams that stay in the up mode and get better with every game are the great teams.

After a very enjoyable career at Auburn, I was thrilled to have a chance at becoming a head coach. I was entering a new world. I declared myself ready at age twenty-six, and I was fortunate that an exciting athletic director at the University of Maine felt the same way. I had learned a great deal in a short time: two years as a graduate assistant and one full year as an assistant at Auburn were very valuable. As I approached being a young head coach, I was proud to be from Maine but had no connections to the AD at Maine, so I had to land the job on my own qualifications. Happily, I did have references from the greats in the game. The late Pat Summit, Joe Ciampi, and the late Sue Gunter were my references. Pat Summit was the best coach in the SEC Conference and in the game. She finished her storied career with the Lady Vols of University of Tennessee, racking up the most career wins of any NCAA women's coach. She was an inspiration.

NCAA postseason success is critical to any coach in terms of growing and finding their ultimate head coaching position. Auburn provided that for me—and more. It was there that I met the man I would marry. John was pursuing his doctorate in economics, and we became friends through a professor friend in the MBA program. John and I enjoyed Auburn very much, but we were ready for more. We were looking for a professorship for John and a head coaching position for me. We were most fortunate that we are able to get the Maine jobs and start a new adventure, both with the basketball program, and also with the economics department at U. Maine.

We married in 1991 on August 18, John's birthday. This fact alone ensured that he would never miss an anniversary, nor have a stand-alone birthday, in his future. It was time for us to start out on our own. Little did we know that it would also be the most transformative time in our lives.

When the University of Maine job was posted, I had immediately taken note with great excitement. There were butterflies in my stomach almost daily, as I thought about the possibilities.

The process was thorough and led by the Maine athletic director Mike Ploszek. I first had a phone interview with a committee. It was interesting to speak on my behalf without seeing the faces of the participants. No zoom calls back then. I was very enthusiastic and had a verbal plan for the Maine women's basketball, which was at the bottom of the league. I earned a trip to Maine for a much more thorough interview. Ironically at this time, John was at a family camping trip. I was sorry to miss the trip, but I had bigger things to do. John and his whole family were eager to learn how things were going. But without cell phones, they had to wait to learn whether I got the job.

The interviews and the campus tour and, of course, meeting with the team went very well. I was certainly relatable, being only four years older than my oldest player. I was offered the job for approximately forty-two thousand dollars a year, almost twice what I was making as an assistant at Auburn.

If I got the job, John planned to teach at Maine, as they were open to the possibility of two hires. I was thrilled and could not wait to get home and tell John. Of course, he was stuck in the mountains and had to find a telephone booth to make the call. He actually reached me at my hotel in Maine. We were headed home to be Maine Black Bears.

John is such an adventurer. Before we moved to Maine, he had a full-time tenured track position at University of Alabama at Birmingham, and we both commuted to our home in Dadeville, almost halfway between our jobs in Birmingham and Auburn. He was ready and willing to move north. I had taken the leap to become a southerner and to marry a man from Tennessee. Now John would find about all about New England and the great people of Maine.

I was young, energized, and proud to be the head coach of women's basketball in my home state at the University of Maine at Orono. I felt an enormous sense of pride, but also pressure to bring the program to the highest level possible. I certainly felt the support of the people in Maine. Mainers are very real folks, and they stand by other Mainers, especially those trying to achieve great things that enhance the pride of the state. Maine can also be a small state, as everyone seems to know each other one way or another. It would also be a safe place to raise a family, something I had personally experienced as a kid.

BELOVED MAINE

I was sitting on the porch in Bangor at our new apartment. I was waiting, at any moment, to see the moving van working its way down our street to our new home. John with his dear father, Mr. Thomas Hooke McCallie, had made the long drive from Auburn. As they crested the hill, at a cautious speed with the U-Haul filled, the reality of our new life and new adventure struck me. We had moved from Auburn to Orono, Maine successfully and with great anticipation of all things Black Bear style.

With John as my partner, I felt confident about all the challenges that head coaching would bring me. John and I shared important wisdom regarding decisions, player relationships, hiring and handling the day-to-day pressures. He is quiet and often in the background, but he is a very good listener. He was invested in all aspects of the program. He was also invested in life in Maine.

Skiing, cross-country skiing, and golf became part of his life. He was introduced to black flies as a steady northern Maine annoyance. They were particularly bad during our first June there together. Just after a long winter with spring finally arriving, daffodils and forsythia in full bloom, the black flies made their presence known. John remarked that he had never experienced such tiny flies that could do so much damage. One had to goop oneself up with oils to prevent the flies from landing and biting at will. Finally, by July, the black flies abated, and the true, very short, Maine summer began.

That season's long days and perfect temperatures made the very dark winters worthwhile.

The first three years of our life in Maine were simply a blur of activity. The women's basketball program was in full swing, and John was busy finding his way through the economics department of the university. Living in Maine was a glorious experience: we thoroughly enjoyed all the seasons. The incredible summers near the ocean, filled with lobster rolls and visits to Acadia National Park, were fantastic. Climbing Mt. Katahdin in the rain, was certainly memorable. The fall was so beautiful, and it was such an incredible and natural transitioning time, with all the leaf colors changing so brilliantly. Even the long winters, that darkened the day in the early hours of the afternoon, were great fun as we worked on downhill skiing and cross-country skiing. But, mostly basketball, of course.

———————

On a snowy winter December evening in 1992 we were able to move into a special house just a few miles from campus. It was warm but snowing, with huge flakes falling rapidly. The neighborhood was completely sugar-coated. It was perfect. The snow crunched under our boots as the exhilaration of moving into our first house together was becoming a reality. With the snow accumulating quickly, and a corner lamp giving us a glow of light, it all seemed so perfect. It was cozy, warm, and so exciting for us to think about raising a family, living on a spacious cul-de-sac, surrounded by great neighbors. Our new house was on Winterhaven Drive, and just like the name suggests, that evening fit the winter wonderland theme perfectly. We were comfortable and beyond excited.

Many cornerstones had fallen into place. Basketball recruiting was going very well, fueling my anticipation for the seasons ahead. The success in our lives, and escaping to the court with games and practices, made for a happy a contented life. The simplicity of the routines and working with the team and staff was most rewarding.

The schedule of a college coach is a full day filled with meetings, practice planning, practice, film sessions for individuals and the team, recruiting, planning for the season travel, flat out getting better with philosophy and technical coaching, motivating everyone daily, holding all accountable, hiring, firing, speaking engagements, fundraising, golf tournaments to reach out to donors and have fun in different environments, special promotional game planning, community outreach and more. We wear many hats as motivators, mentors, leaders, public speakers, sports psychologists at times, and, of course, coaching day to day.

Coaching is a lifestyle 24/7 on-call, and a coach must be prepared to deal with any player, staff or recruiting issues around the clock. If all things are going well, taking off one day a week is possible. My husband used to joke with me that on my one day *off* I was always watching film or writing up practice for the next day!

Assembling a great team hinges largely on great recruiting. In this day and age, social media has made it so that recruits want a lot of attention—daily, or even throughout the day. There is no such thing as once-a-week call. Writing letters is still good and can elevate a head coach with recruits, but the texts and calls are still the most important. In-person off-campus visits are key as well. The Zoom world—especially during the covid outbreak—have forced virtual home visits that are a lot of fun and could change the culture of recruiting for the future. And it is a huge money saver.

Within a normal season, a head coach must meet with and placate parents and boosters who support the team. You also must hire and mentor a staff, including assistant coaches. Then of course, there are the everyday tribulations of players who need guidance, attention and countless hours of coaching. Plus maintaining healthy team dynamics.

Teaching almost seems, at times, a smaller part of the of the job, but certainly is the most enjoyable. Practice and games are truly everyone's favorite things, and what I miss most to this day is my interactions with the players. I loved the prep and the speed and quickness of running a game like practice.

Of course, recruiting and scheduling are the foundations to any program. Recruiting great talent is obviously a key, but matching the right schedule to your team's ability to mix challenging games with others, helps balance the schedule to get the team ready for the conference season. Building confidence in your team and challenging them at the same time in practice and the games is a day-to-day process. There can be no shortage of motivation among individuals and teams. Most times the best players want to be coached hard and often want more instruction, extra work, and film review. Other times, the best players want to rely on their talent, or will limit themselves by not improving their weaker skills. Each player must be motivated differently as she grows through her four-year career. This is a tall task for any coach. Staying technical with the right balance of reason and emotions is a key. Diving into the process of getting better is the focus. When a player bucks you on process, or refuses to become a better defender or a better free-throw shooter, then the coach must circle back and try to begin again with a different approach.

There is no substitute for hard work, extra time prepping, and repetition. Great players have a great work ethic and sometimes have a higher future image of themselves than the coach does. That player is the most fun player to coach. They love getting better and they do not limit themselves to any amount of success. They understand the process and submerge themselves in their own bubble. Of course, the best elite players do all of this while making everyone around them play better. These players are the most special and make the most impact on the program.

I was young and eager to prove my value as a good head coach. I pushed for perfection and covered all details. I stayed in the office late into the evenings with a pepperoni pizza from Pat's. (Pat's pizza was like no other.) Coaches sometimes eat erratically and poorly, so Pat helped get me through with tasty snacks on busy nights.

But I wish I could have told my young self to slow down, because I was determined to bring our home-state university to places it had never gone. I had an almost singular focus on the university and my team. The idea of pausing to enjoy the moment was not natural to me at that time. Pausing did not seem like a viable option. I became a great *doer* at the expense of becoming a great *listener.*

At a speaking engagement I would anticipate my ideas without regard to really hearing the supporters. I had much to say and sound-bytes were more frequent than just casual listening. Too much politician! I was just wanting to get things done and get to that space of success, wherever it may be for the future. I was young and had a plan, a vision and an idea about how to run the program. Because it was the first year of the staff and my first year as a head coach, I had to set the tone and teach my philosophy.

———————

I was determined to improve the Maine program, from the bottom to the top, as soon as possible. There is no doubt that I made some rookie mistakes, some of which nobody realized at the time. There is a certain freedom to being brand-new with a learning curve for everyone, especially with a rookie head coach. Some recruiting choices were not prudent, the whole staff learned how to spend money properly, and boundaries had to be set for me and the young staff.

One of our biggest mistakes came early, as the result of a scheduling error: an assistant coach had scheduled too many games. We had gone from 9-20 to 20-7 and won the league outright. But because we had played too many games, the conference coaches voted to kick us, the top seed, out of the NAC tournament. Just like that, our chances were nixed to play in the NCAA tourney. That was truly the costliest mistake of that season, and one that stings to this day. But basketball is a game of mistakes, so how we cope and care with accountability and forward-thinking is the key. The process always moves on in good and bad times.

Goal setting can be important. But as I grew in coaching, I began to understand the true value of the overall coaching process. This thinking indicates that a team and staff focus on the small pieces daily. When a team is buried in the process, they tend to look at the scoreboard less, and play each game with a fluidity. Mistakes are a part of the process. The great executions and the poor decisions, rather than the outcomes, make up this journey of process-driven playing, for every practice, every day and every game. Until my time coaching at MSU, I did not completely orient myself with such thinking. Early in my career, I was more of an outcome-driven coach bound to cut down the nets and think ahead of myself, in terms of what it takes to get there, and perhaps skip a few solid teaching steps and philosophy along the way.

My eight years at Maine were a whirlwind of energy and accomplishment. But I paid a price, as I was unable to appreciate the deeper subtleties of coaching and life. Where was *the pause,* the ability to be still and savor successes or learnings? Productivity is a wonderful thing. Being productive makes one incredibly happy and fulfilled. But purely chasing productivity can blind us to the very details that can allow us to be more efficient and see the bigger picture. For that to happen, we have to make time for it.

For John and me, our whirlwind lives sped up even more when our firstborn came into this world on August 31, 1994. Maddie came into the world, eyes open with a brightness and curiosity. She quickly looked about and had an eagerness to getting started in her little world. She never cried upon her arrival. I believe all parents say something like this, but in this case, it was true. She was simply ready to go and begin her own adventure. I had been very active, swimming daily and playing golf, during my pregnancy. The day before I gave birth, I walked nine holes while pulling my cart in the early evening. The activity seemed to help my labor tremendously. I had roughly forty-five minutes of pushing before Madeline Clark arrived at around eight on the next morning.

The day was beautiful. There were no clouds, just a bright crisp blue surrounding us. I looked out the window, while holding my newborn daughter, with a sense of immense joy and pride. The Kennebec River was glistening from the bright and clear sunshine. Fall was in the air already. The natural childbirth had seemed to spike my endorphins in a way that made life seem surreal and richly full. There was no happier moment to me. True and utter bliss is when you know you are in exactly the right place, at the right time. I was there, nursing Maddie and capturing one of the most significant moments in my life. However, Maddie's birth did not slow me down nearly enough. I was back working the very next day, first at home and then back to the office later that week. I took pride in being able to pump my milk two-fisted while talking on the phone or watching game film. I pumped at home and at work, and I nursed Maddie there, too. There was a constant flow of action while I attended to Maddie and pursued my coaching desires and obligations.

All coaches have their own stories of juggling work and personal lives. The profession truly is about the business of developing people. I have dedicated thirty years of my life to this wonderful development piece and loved every minute of it. I never anticipated that being a young head coach at twenty-six would be so incredibly challenging. I was too much in *go* mode to even think about it.

BREAKDOWN

Anxiety can come in all forms, particularly to a working new mother who craves routine and planning. Of course, being organized is the half the battle to thriving with baby and family. Maddie had been so easy and simple to raise in her first year. Frozen packages of pumped milk were plentiful and stored in the freezer. Feeding Maddie was a moment of peace for all. She took to her bottle well and John and I were gaining confidence as new parents. The jar food, complete with veggies, was very helpful. Sweet potato purée never looked and tasted so good to her growing palate. Everything, at first, appeared easy for this new mom.

Soon the obvious—but not so obvious to this new mom—took hold: Maddie would need to eat more adult-like food. This was natural for any growing child. But I was neither a cook nor creatively equipped to come up with quick and nutritious meals. So far, basketball had consumed my life. At no point had I ever spent time in the kitchen. I was simply not interested.

I gave Maddie a bath each night to anchor her bedtime routine. But something as basic as preparing the meals for both Maddie and John overwhelmed me. John, by contrast, was a modern man with cooking skills of his own. He did not share my meal-preparer anxiety. I wish I had recognized at the time that preparing food for your family can be a blessing that provides special quality time with your young child or spouse. Once again, I was manically pursuing my coaching career, speeding through life, working countless hours and not pausing to savor the other important things around me. At the time, I could not conceive of slowing down or taking a break from work obligations. In some ways, it's quite humorous for me to reflect back on this time as a high-anxiety life. I could whip up a team through practice and games, but I was stumped and intimidated by preparing meals for my young daughter and husband. This almost hyperactive style of life, with constant lists and deadlines in your mind, not to mention being a new mom, breeds a life of immediacy taken too far. This pace can be unhealthy, and combined with other work-life stressors, can bring on a frenetic activity ripe for mental health challenges. The situation and triggers can be critical factors in the evolution of the unquiet mind.

As Maddie's first birthday came and went, fall arrived in fine fashion. My anxiety was subtle, but percolating. John was very supportive, and keeping his sense of humor about the realities of our busy life. Regardless of the smiles and gentle joking, I felt an overwhelming sense of inadequacy as a wife and parent. Structure has always been important in my life, and going with the flow has never been my strong suit. I now realize that maternal confidence grows over time.

September and October of 1995 exacerbated my feelings of inadequacy. I remember that time clearly. It was truly exciting for me, professionally. I was thrilled to be building a special program with primarily student-athletes from Maine and the northeast. We recruited some very special student-athletes during my eight-year tenure. I knew, in taking the job as head coach, that Maine is truly a basketball state. Everyone was watching and anticipating our climb.

I was fortunate to have one of the nation's leading talents on my roster, a woman who would help lift the team and me personally.

We recruited a future Maine star in Cindy Blodgett. One of the most heralded high school players in the history of Maine and nationally, Cindy was the nation's leading scorer for two years, and broke all boundaries relative to life in Maine as a basketball star. She is one of few individuals who was, and still is, recognized to this day by just her first name. She was a legend in high school, winning four straight state championships.

Our relationship started while I recruited her on the phone, still the record for my longest recruiting call in twenty-eight years of coaching. We chatted for four straight hours and I missed an entire dinner and evening with friends on the ocean that night. To me, it was worth every bit of that effort, and that conversation was precedent-setting for our long-term relationship. We had to convince Cindy to see the value in playing for Maine as a national contender. She had been recruited by many big conference schools, but we were building something special at Maine, and she needed to know that she could be a catalyst to making history.

After Cindy's first year at Maine, I was approached by another university to coach at their school after my record-setting year at Maine. While John and I appreciated the athletic director from the West Coast school very much, we did not feel the fit would be good for the school. We were still very committed to Maine, but issues had arisen that had to be addressed. Budgets and salaries were low, and women's basketball at Maine needed to catch up to the market value of what was happening nationwide.

We had begun enjoying sellout crowds—over five thousand per game. Cindy led the charge and shared the success with great teammates as the program received overwhelming support from the community. But I felt strongly that I needed to make many changes within the program, and I could use a visit to the West Coast school as a bargaining tool with my administration. I met with Cindy to share with her that I could not give her all the details. I asked her to trust me with this process and trust that the program could benefit.

Cindy is a fiercely loyal person, and she accepted my explanation. So that weekend, John and I were off and away to explore a new opportunity. It is always interesting how the market, along with another potential coaching opportunity, can change the dynamics and your negotiating position at your current school. This trend, of being recruited and looking at schools, continued throughout my career and helped my current school catch up to the market value of our accomplishments. And it seemed to be the only way to get the full attention of athletic directors. Coaches of women's basketball find that part of our work and leadership is to continue to grow our programs in every way. If that meant getting on a plane to take a look around, then so be it.

Upon our return to the airport in Maine, we were met by media who speculated that we were going to take the job on the West Coast. Even though some media tried to imply directly to Cindy that I would be taking the job, I gave no indication of our plans to anyone. I was ready to meet with the president and AD to talk about more support for our program. And as we had hoped, administrative shifts were made, including salaries and budget increases for women's basketball. Changes were arranged. Cindy and the team knew I was committed to them. Our bond solidified in an incredibly special way.

This experience matured our relationship further, and helped me and Cindy both deal with my ultimate challenge—an active coach diagnosed with a mood disorder. In addition to Cindy, we had tremendous senior leadership from a passionate and truth-telling talented player in Steph Guidi. We were on our way to creating a top-level program and aiming to rise in the North Atlantic Conference. Developing my current team and talent inherited by a coach and staff, and combining that with great recruiting, set our framework for success. Some coaches want only players they recruited, believing others will not be loyal to them. My experience has been the players are resilient and will learn and grow as the coach motivates them and trusts in their talent.

———————

As the conference name changed to America East, our success stayed steady and dominant.

The annual Midnight Madness was in the air. We were opening the season in the basketball and hockey facility at the University of Maine, Alfond Arena. The evening was a celebration for both the men's and women's teams. The band was playing and introductions were matched with music and grand entrances for all the players. I was enjoying some dance moves at center court with our men's coach. It was a celebration for the fans, too, starting at midnight, to welcome the official practice season. The evening was memorable and indicative of many good things to come.

Overshadowing the jubilation of the new season, however, were extenuating circumstances at work. There were problems at U of Maine stemming from a lack of funding for compliance support and education. This support in adhering strictly to NCAA rules is pivotal to the success of a well-engineered athletic department. Those in compliance have a tall task in keeping the coaches educated in the latest rule changes governing their sport, along with enforcing rules and regulations set for the by the NCAA. Investigations by the NCAA are very disruptive to all athletic departments. Our hockey program was under investigation. It behooves a university to put forth the funds to create a solid compliance department. In the midst of the troubles, the athletic director who hired me suffered the unfair blow of being let go, and I refused to partake in the processes of hiring his replacement.

This was a very unfortunate and distressing time for me and our family. We loved the man and athletic director who hired and believed in us. Mike was excellent and very well received.

The program, the team and I, were very fortunate to have great support from Steve and Tabby King, graduates of the University of Maine, and other Maine fans and alumni who were excited for us to build the program. We needed them to guide us through those unsettling times. Stephen is a world-renown author and his wife, Tabitha, is a writer as well. They both took a special interest in our teams, which delighted us all. There was a time when an opponent team asked to meet Steve. The University of Wisconsin players and staff were beyond thrilled when, after a tournament game, Steve agreed to say hello. Those were special times of great support and Maine people embracing our program. The table was set for great things for Maine women's basketball.

One day, while I was taking my daily masters swim in the university pool, I was interrupted by an administrative assistant from the athletic director's office. Suddenly, I was being pulled out of the water and told to quickly report to the interim athletic director who had requested my immediate presence. Dripping wet, and still in my swimsuit and a T-shirt, I hustled to his office. He immediately and clearly asserted that I did not support him. He began to suggest there could be some NCAA compliance rules that he, and the administration, could look into regarding donor involvement in our program. I knew there was nothing to his threat. The donors and supporters were great people doing everything right, *legally* supporting the University of Maine in all ways.

At that time, I began to realize that this was a form of intimidation. That experience made me worry about the support I could receive in the future. That intimidating exchange stayed with me, adding to the stress of coaching a team with high expectations while being an attentive mother and wife. I was a rookie at this pressure game, and I felt like one.

Athletic department politics were not my strong suit. I proceeded to get overly concerned about the future before the season even began. An emotional insomnia became part of my life. My sleep patterns shifted. I was restless with the excitement of the team, my mind swirling, sometimes out of control, thrusting me toward the hypo-manic state called *mania*.

————————————

Mania provides you with an incredible sense of energy and an upbeat positive attitude that makes you think everything around you is geared toward you, and that you can do anything. In that way, it is almost a hyper curse of energy and an inflated sense of self. Your mind operates very quickly. You have irrational thoughts, including thinking that the songs on the radio are meant just for you. You feel as if everything you experience has an underlying meaning directed only at you. It is an incredible feeling of exhilaration, energy, and brain flow that, despite its clear issues, is indeed most attractive for creativity and productivity.

Simply put, your brain is on overdrive. You are flooded with ideas and thoughts continually. They almost shoot right at you to the point of making you feel that everything is urgent. You are fully engaged, and you anticipate conversations at a rapid speed. Truly, you feel as if you're flying through life—in a most positive way.

In coaching, the great measures in determining a team's outcomes are intensity, immediacy, and intelligence. In sports, this is called the "I Test." It's simple, but very provocative when assessing a team's ability to commit to the process of improvement. My personal I Test results indicated that I was overreactive and churning, at a breaking point. I had to slow down and dedicate myself to my own process. Too much immediacy, and too much intensity, surrounded my world. Intelligence, and making the right choices, would have to take over.

The catch, of course, is that your sleeping habits become erratic and often sleep is very difficult. With less sleep over the course of days or weeks, your brain starts to burn ideas too fast. You are not totally cogent relative to what you talk about and your reasoning. Your brain is working too hard to keep up with your thoughts.

When you are completely hypo-manic, you begin to run out of gas physically and mentally as your thinking becomes disoriented. Medicine is the only way to slow down your very unquiet mind. It is a lonely feeling to realize your brain is completely in charge and affecting you this way. You cannot believe that your mind has taken charge. You have truly "lost" your mind. This realization brings about great fear: fear of all the unknowns and how you will care for yourself during your life; fear about telling your family or sharing information with anybody; fear about your employer finding out and somehow choosing a way to discriminate, around mental illness only, because many just do not understand and themselves fear the consequences of the situation. There's such a stigma that people recoil with fear. Corrective medication can affect your ability to have a child, and can take its toll over a period of time and cause physical harm to your body. Throughout my early coaching years, many of those realities came to fruition for me. Eventually, one related life and medication challenge was to prove significant. My years of stability would be challenged during my episodes in Maine.

———————————

At the University of Maine, my reduced sleep seemed like a great new way of life. I could plan and organize my day and simultaneously search out the best plays for my talented team. It was a perfect time to think and plan. It seemed almost meditative. Three or four hours, or no sleep at all, appeared to be sufficient in this new life I was leading. All my life I had been an eight-hour heavy sleeper. This new reality, although it looked like increased efficiency in living, was not normal.

John, at first, was not aware that I was sleeping less. My mood was high and positive. I was feeling so productive in every way. Our life with Maddie was going well with John shouldering the larger burden of meal planning. I delighted in taking care of Maddie as I was no longer nursing her, and she was a precocious one-year-old growing up in her new world. I was happy and had found a work-life balance.

But even with my personal aura of steadiness, John did not know what to do when my behavior became excitable. I would talk at a faster rate, and existed in a strange state of my mind, my thoughts moving faster than normal. The thoughts were sharp and pointed, but assertive and always jumping around in my head. It was a pleasant high feeling, and I felt as if I could accomplish anything. My euphoric mind-altering enthusiasm was growing.

"I remember walking across campus with you to grab a bite to eat," my husband recounted. "You were excited and talking rapidly about the news coverage and all the possibilities. Your words and expressed dreams were not too far-fetched, but they were grandiose, as you talked about Final Fours and a national title. The conversation was motivating, but filled with so much energy. Euphoric in nature, and greatly confident in delivery. You had me believing . . . and then really wondering."

Expectations that season were high, fueled by my euphoria and the media hype that fed off of it. I loved the attention and hype at first, but would later come to dislike it and even avoid that kind of inflated sentiments, then and throughout my career.

Later, as I grew as a coach, I learned to dismiss media predictions. I learned that preseason polls are much like a beauty pageant: it is only what others think of you, from a superficial sense, and evaluation, and that's all. The only poll that ever matters is the one at the end of the season. Media can tell great stories, but miss the deeper nature of a team and what's important. The fan mentality of being a poll- and prediction-follower conflicts with the concept of teaching the evolution as a team, game by game, with complete focus on each step in the building process. All teams and individuals in sport must concentrate on the action of getting better, without predictions or hypotheticals. Getting caught up in the hype and the expectations it creates can be destructive.

John, recalled the hypo-manic episode that day. It was clearly leading me down a dangerous but enthralling path. I was generating excitement instead of focusing on my true instincts about my team's prospects. My brain was busy altering, and creating, a grandiose personal world.

———————

During this first episode, John knew he had to act, but he did not know what he was facing with me. My sister came to Orono during this time because John reached out for her help with me. My personality was different, and I was acting so strangely. My thoughts were racing and my speech was too fast. John felt enormously responsible to rectify the situation through talking with me gently. He was not familiar with what he saw, and he sensed it was not good.

At work, I was recruiting at a rapid-fire pace. My conversations with prospects flowed easily and my productivity in the evenings was excellent—at least from my perspective. Not so with John. One night, I was on the phone with a recruit from home, the TV was on—and I told the recruit that the TV was speaking directly to me. John overheard that exchange and immediately took the phone from me, telling the recruit that I was having a playful and silly moment. He intercepted the problem, and made light of it. But down deep, he was growing increasingly concerned. He knew that trouble was looming, and he was not quite sure how to fix it.

We did sign that recruit, despite my episode. Jamie Cassidy became one of the finest post players to play at Maine and in the nation. She led us to numerous conference championships and great success in the NCAA tournament as well. But despite on-the-court successes, my mental state deteriorated off the court. John initially used a gynecological appointment to seek help. We went together to see Dr. Joe, an excellent physician who had helped bring Maddie into the world. We sat in his office, talking about seemingly nothing too important. My behavior was erratic and revealing. Dr. Joe and John sat patiently as I asked questions, one on top of another, with a fiery and rapid pace. I was happy, but delusional. My questions to Dr. Joe were without concern or connection to the discussion. I was also a bit frustrated, because everything was fine in my eyes: why were we really at this appointment? Odd, inappropriate thoughts about their motivations came to my head, and I was confused and ready to blame John and Dr. Joe for this unnecessary appointment.

I was a good mom, and the visit started affably, but shortly my thoughts evolved into a sense of paranoia and fear of the unknown. John and I had never been to my gynecologist's office together—at least, not for what was supposed to be a routine check-up. The two of them seemed to be talking about me, and around me. They both looked at me quizzically. I felt uneasy and anxious. Eyes do not lie. I was ready to leave. When I left the doctor's office, I was still unaware of exactly what our conversation was about, or the exact reason for our going in the first place.

I later learned that the idea of a special hospital in Bangor was suggested to John as an option to discover the cause of my apparent lack of mental wellness. I was oblivious and even dismissive of my state of mind. But John had formulated a plan. The day after the office visit, John led me to our car, saying that we were going for a ride to enjoy the beautiful day, and that we would be back very soon. I was delighted to be going for a drive with John, to have some quality time with my husband on a beautiful Maine day.

I can remember my sister standing in the driveway, holding Maddie, as we got into the car. Maddie's response to the odd scenario was telling. As she was held in Carolyn's arms, she screamed and cried in a way I had never seen before. I just could not understand why she could possibly be so upset. She loved her Aunt Carolyn, and she was generally very happy, and certainly comfortable with her aunt, but she seemed to know that something was very wrong and that her mommy was going away. I did not respond as a nurturing mother at that moment. I smiled broadly and with confidence, and proceeded to simply focus on my own happiness—actually mania—at the moment. Children's natural sense of danger or unknowns seemed to explain her behavior. But in my manic state, I assumed Maddie would be okay.

MANIC

There was a cool fall breeze and bright sunshine on that October day in 1995. As John and I drove, I kept asking him where exactly where we were going. He said only that we were going to a place to get some special help. I trusted John, and thought he was referring to himself—thinking that he needed help in some way. With a smile, I was more than eager to help John.

In my happy state and as a supportive wife, I painted a picture in my head that John was not okay. I kept quiet to support him, but gave him smiles of reassurance, even though my euphoric state did not allow for real empathy toward John. I just looked out the window at the gorgeous day and continued to wonder about him. Of course, the reality was that John was fine. He wanted me to enjoy the ride, which was a decoy to our destination. He anticipated I would put up resistance when I understood that the problem was with me.

When we went inside the hospital in Bangor, although I still did not understand why we were there, I eagerly and inquisitively followed John. We were directed to a waiting room. I saw some children's toys on the floor, and thought it was fabulous. I thought it would be so much fun to sit on the floor, just like a child, and play with these toys. John gave me a funny look but said nothing. As he observed me, enjoying myself immensely playing with toys, his worry heightened. When they called for us, John must have experienced some relief. We took an elevator to the second floor. As we stepped out of the elevator, I still wondered what John needed and how my being there could help him.

We were greeted by a couple of doctors in the hallway. They said the ward we were on would be a good place for me. *Me? Not John!?* I was incredulous. I started to get very agitated. Then I heard the doctor tell John that he could go, and I was to stay. I became feverishly panicked and hyper when John began to leave. The hallway door shut behind me, and I quickly realized it did not open from the inside. I banged on those doors hard, as if my fists were bionic and would allow me to break through. Then I ran to find the nearest window, banging and pleading to get out as I tried to open each sealed window over and over again.

At first, the doctors just let me bang and bang harder as I tried to escape. I found myself sprinting down the hallway looking for other possible escape methods. Again, the doctors watched as I continued to sprint, dodge other patients, looking for an escape route. Eventually, they decided to act.

The doctors and nurses approached aggressively and quickly. I fought even harder. I fought them all; I screamed, I yelled, I punched, I kicked. I did everything to keep them away from me. They pushed me into a room as I resisted. But they were overpowering, pinning my arms and wrists and forcing my head onto a pillow on the nearest bed. They flipped me onto my stomach. I was absolutely terrified. They pulled down my pants quickly, and the next thing I knew there was a piercing pain as something was injected into my body. Almost immediately I was out—completely knocked out. Fully surrendered, I still did not know why I was there.

Many years later, a doctor colleague agreed that it was entirely unnecessary for me to have been handled in such a physical and demeaning manner. I certainly hope methods are different today.

Later, when I awoke in my room, I was startled and fearful and did not understand why I was in this room alone. I was a thirty-year-old head coach, wife, and a mother of one beautiful child. Life was good, in my mind. I was successful and happy. Why had John, my trusted and loyal spouse, done this to me? I was cognizant enough to know that I had been committed to a mental health institution.

Eventually the staff told me to take a shower and clean up. I found their directions to be completely unacceptable, perhaps evil, and I feared they might hurt me again, so I absolutely refused to shower. I remained curled up on my bed, wondering how I would get myself out of this hospital. I was a popular, young, excited new coach in a quiet dark room with no one to talk to about my surreal experience. One day earlier, I was home feeling happy, perhaps too much so, but safe in my family world.

———————

I had fallen asleep again and when I awoke, a ray of light shined through the window that was small and uninspiring. I lay there, curled in a ball, trying to remember everything. My brain was foggy. I began to take note of where I was, and search for any clue that could lead me to freedom. I was determined to remember it all. I was going to figure this out. I was also determined, and continued to forgo a shower as requested by the nurse. My hair was matted and disheveled, and my skin was sticky from dried sweat. Yet, I wanted to maintain my sense of control and dignity in this new place that frightened me. But there was a distinct antiseptic smell that permeated the stale air. The room was stuffy, too warm, and marked by body odor. Following nurses' orders made me feel powerless, too agreeable, and an enabler in their bizarre plan.

In time I was taken to see the doctor who spoke to me in a gentle and calming tone.

He explained that I had experienced an episode they believed to be mania. At that time, I was not sure what it all meant. The word "bipolar" was suggested as a possible diagnosis. I was told that I would stay in the hospital to be evaluated, and then for some time to recover with medication. I would participate in group sessions with other patients. This thought terrified me further. At that exact point in the meeting, I had resolved myself to find a way out of this building.

I was returned to my small room with the dreaded shower. I was again encouraged to clean up and get ready for the day. Once again, I refused. I remained in my clothes as long as I could. There was a change of clothing, at some point, so that I could officially join the ranks of the committed patients. The patients sported light blue pajama-type pants and tops. I was told I was going to a group session with other patients to start my therapy. This was truly a surreal and defining moment for me.

I sat at a conference table with approximately eight other patients. They all looked very odd, and the mental states of some seemed more severe than others. I wondered where I fell on the spectrum. Some stared blankly into the distance. Some were mumbling and talking out loud. One person was having a conversation with an imaginary friend. Another stared at me coldly and directly. I wondered if they knew I was the new admit to further crowd their world.

I cannot remember exactly what was said during that session. Oddly, I felt I could relate to some of the faces and how their minds seemed to be working. I looked about and I wondered about their stories. How did they get into this hospital, and what were the reasons for their illnesses? I sat quietly. I refused to talk. I couldn't make sense of it. I was skeptical, and angry. I felt an incredible loss of privacy. How could I be there? Sharing and talking with strangers was exactly what I did not want to do. I shut down completely. I simply refused to utter a word. I stared at the nurse who was coordinating the group. I just stared at her without even a blink.

———————

After the session, I returned to my room and decided that I would have to do something—and soon. From a pay phone, I called my husband and my sister Carolyn and asked them to come get me. Of course, they told me that the people at the hospital would help me. I was very frustrated with this answer. I felt angry and betrayed, as if my family had turned on me at an exceedingly difficult time. They said that they would come visit, but they would not bring Maddie. I got very emotional, mystified, and wary about their reluctance for me to see Maddie.

Later that afternoon, with smiles and a board game to play, John and my sister arrived. I did not look well after the stress of not sleeping and not showering. I refused to allow my body to be touched. As John walked down the hall he tried to hug and comfort me. I pushed him away, breaking free of his grasp, and I became enraged with them both. Why had they done this to me, and how could they expect me to stay in this hospital? My daughter and my team needed me.

I began yelling loudly at John and Carolyn for double-crossing me in a way that I could not forgive. I pulled my wedding ring off and threw it at John. I was clear to me that I could never forgive him. Carolyn was shocked by my behavior. She backed up hesitantly, her eyes welling up with tears. She did not say a word, but instead looked on in disbelief as she observed my actions and heard those words of desperate loathing. I told them to get out. I told them to leave and not come back. I did not want any visitors in this space.

The sunny day darkened. I realized that I would be spending the night in that awful place. I chose not to eat my dinner. I chose not to participate in anything at all. My mind was still working rapid-fire as I decided who I would call next. My players were on my mind repeatedly. I knew they would find out and be wondering about their coach. Steve and Tabby King had been strong supporters of our program and the team, and they were aware of my current situation. Tabby had written a book chronicling Cindy Blodgett's high school career. Calling them seemed like a good plan. I felt a kindred spirit with all Maine folks.

The nurses had taken my belongings away, but I had managed

to hang on to my address and contact book. These were days long before cell phones, Facetime, and computers were used readily and easily. I found myself in a quiet corner and began to use the pay phone. I first called all my players to let them know everything would be okay. This only scared them more as I explained that I had been admitted to the hospital against my will.

Later, I would learn that four of my players—Steph, Catherine, Stacia and Cindy—had come to the hospital in the evening during my short stay there. They were trying to find a way to sneak into the hospital and find me. They wanted to know what was happening to their coach. To this day, I have always been grateful and moved by their care and courage. They were all incredible strong women with big hearts.

Steph was a four-year player for me and had committed to Maine prior to my arrival. I was very fortunate to coach Steph Guidi, Catherine Gallant and Stacia Rustad all four years. Steph had always stood apart with her incredible energy and authenticity. Her fire and passion were critical each year she played. I loved her tenacity and fight, which was exhibited in many ways in practice and in games. Her intensity and immediacy about the game were only matched by her loyalty to her teammates and staff members. She was a thinker by nature and trusted her instincts.

I have always been amazed by her keen sense of understanding and empathy. We shared a special moment when Steph offered me a picture of herself from high school. I looked at the picture in utter disbelief. Steph was significantly heavier before she came to Maine.

"Yeah, I was the fat kid on the floor that everyone made fun of," she said, except they could not tease Steph too much because she could really play. The sharing of that picture spoke to Steph's truth about herself and about others. I was struck by her frankness and ability to make such an incredible change in her life to become an outstanding Division I athlete. Her wisdom, empathy and leadership would stand tall at a critical time in my life. As the events unfolded during my first episode, Steph was a star. Her words regarding being a part of my first episode are beyond inspiring.

"We had a team meeting with the assistant coaches that day and they explained to us that Coach P had been admitted to the hospital for exhaustion and that she was going to be fine and that she had admitted herself.

"I did not believe one word of that, so I pressed them to give us the truth. They said that was the truth but proceeded to tell us that if she tries to contact us that we should say exactly what they told us from a script. Something along the lines of, 'You're going to be okay, Coach P. You need this break and the rest before the season gets going. This is the best thing for you.'

"Later that evening, I was asleep, and the phone rang around one. I knew exactly who it was and answered. Coach P whispered on the phone, almost as though she did not want to get caught, and said, 'Steph, it's Coach P. I am at the hospital. They are keeping me here against my will and I need to get out.'

"I tried the script asserted by the assistants and administration. Coach P could read right through my words."

"That's bullshit, Steph. Now you go use that tough attitude and find a way to get me out."

Cindy also received a late-night call for help. I was whispering to her over the phone to avoid nurses.

"Cindy, I need your help. I am being held in the hospital against my will. Please come get me outta here."

Steph, Cindy and other fellow seniors on the team were determined to seek out the real story and decided to visit the hospital for answers. They were refused entry, but rustled around looking in a few windows to find their coach. Then they were told not to contact me when I was released.

"When I found out Coach was discharged, I bee-lined it to her home to visit her," Steph said. "It was calm, a calm like I had never experienced before with Coach. We sat, we visited quietly, we hugged, and I told her I loved her unconditionally. Her team loved her unconditionally and we were going to support her however she needed and in any capacity."

The wisdom of these calls and getting my team so involved was clearly ill-advised and unfair. My mind was operating out of desperation. I put a lot of pressure on a young person early that morning.

Steph and Cindy felt helpless. Cindy went back to the dorm very concerned and disillusioned.

"I was young and immature in many ways," she would recall later in life. "But, I felt very protective of Coach when I returned. I didn't ever speak directly to her about how I felt, but it was something I thought of often during the rest of my playing career."

Incredible thinking for a young person. The implicit nature of communication and belief was truly a part of my overall success in getting beyond my illness. But, learning these thoughts from Cindy, and other players, now gives me chills of guilt and responsibility for putting them in such a difficult situation. So many years later, there is still a clear rawness to the memories. The conversations and emails brought a sober reality to me. My players, too, had wounds that remained from their experiences during the time.

"To me, many people may have folded under the circumstances," Steph said. "Some may have quit. Some might even think of transferring. Some may, and did, call for a coaching change. There was no way we would ever let that happen. That season we went 24-6, undefeated in the conference, beat No. 9 Alabama in January, 75-73 and earned a seed in the NCAA tournament. We had our coach throughout and never looked back."

———

News had traveled fast in a small town like Bangor and Orono, and my privacy was at a premium. I was, after all, a public figure leading the vaunted women's basketball team. However, I did have a sense of peace and support from fellow Mainers. I experienced a sense of grace and hope from many of them. Perhaps some of the more critical folks from outside would eventually understand.

The actions of the women/players who came to liberate me had sent me a clear message—I was their coach. They were committed to our dreams. They refused to sit back and let the administration take hold of the situation as rumors swirled about my fate with the school and the team. Some people had believed that my days were numbered as the head coach. But the players were in control and ready to stand by me. I have never forgotten their loyalty and pride in all that we were doing.

While adults in charge were lost in the political wave of the circumstances, the players were already moving forward. To them it was simple. "Coach P," as I am known in the basketball world, needed their support while she got better. To this day, these women are almost solely responsible for my long tenure in coaching. At any point, amongst the confusion and guesswork, my career could have been cut short. There was parental concern, but little interference with the players' support for me. The team, with such great leadership, pushed hard to support me, reminding all of their commitment.

The athletic director and university president were trying to cope with the unknowns. They had pondered replacing me just as the season was about to begin. At the time, I was emboldened by my team, and looking to take things day-to-day as I had found my way through this bizarre puzzle. Thanks to my players, I stuck around, and we would have many championships to come. I was most fortunate to have a long coaching career.

———————————

Back at the hospital when I looked in my contact lists, one of the numbers I found was Steve's number. I would make a desperation move. I had no sense of propriety or respect for his time. I felt bold hope and ready to do whatever it took to get out.

My mind raced, but I kept my voice to a whisper. I wanted no one to overhear. Steve repeated what John and Carolyn had suggested to me. His words were warm and simple. Stay put, and let the people at the hospital help me. Completely off-topic, but related to my condition, I abruptly asked him to send me a deep-dish pizza. Steve knew nothing about that exact type of. pizza, but my mind had jolted back to my Chicago days when I was in college, and the fun we used to have as a team at Northwestern enjoying the Chicago specialty. Of course, in reality it had no place or relevancy in that conversation. Random memories and bizarrely timed recollections are part of the deal with mania. Interestingly, later that evening, a pizza did arrive for me, sent via Tabby and Steve. Steve wrote me a note to encourage me to let the people in the hospital help me. He assured me that everything would be okay. He did write in the note with a sense of humor, "Sorry, no deep dish."

I did eat that pizza. It represented something safe to me, and reassuring. It was something from the outside world, something uncontaminated. I was so grateful for the meal and gesture. I had a taste of progress in a small, but motivating, way. There had to be a way to find an exit. After all, in my cycling mind, this had been such a big mistake. I told myself, *Joanne, think. You have rights and responsibilities. THEY cannot take them away from you against your will.*

My small experiences with the law, from my interning days in Chicago, came to mind. I needed someone to believe me. I even felt I could sue the hospital for malpractice. Big talk for a swirling mind, but it all made sense to me.

I was more on my own than I could ever imagine. I began to look about the ward more carefully and see if there was any way to sneak out when the doors occasionally opened. Nothing seemed possible. There was too much security: the doors did not open without a code, and the windows were thick and unbreakable.

My mind quickly moved to a neighbor back home who lived

across the street, and who happened to be an experienced attorney. He was good man, and he had been reliable and kind. I found his number and called to tell him that I had been committed without my consent. I told him I was being held against my will and that I needed to get out. My neighbor had no reason to disbelieve me. He was very empathetic as he sorted through the story. I was very convincing as I told him that the whole ordeal was just one big mistake. My family needed me back at home. My neighbor began to use his legal abilities to get a court order releasing me from the hospital.

Of course, I asked him not to contact anybody in my family. I knew that if he did, I would remain captive. I was so grateful to him for proceeding with my case so quickly. Before I knew it, he was representing me at the hospital. He made some incredibly good points about me being held against my will.

I called my brother-in-law, Brian, and asked him to come get me. I quickly explained to him that an attorney had made it possible for me to leave. Brian was very concerned. I also made the story slightly unclear and rushed. The exhilaration of getting into Brian's car felt like an incredible victory. I was a warrior captured in a foreign land, now freed from the tyrants trying to take over my life.

―――――――――――――

It was yet another gorgeous fall day. Not a cloud in the sky, and the sun shining brightly. The leaves had turned different shades of red, orange, and yellow. Brian and I spoke very few words on the drive home. I suspect he was wondering if he was doing the right thing. As the wind was blowing with the convertible top open, the undeniable beauty of the cool crisp fall had settled in and given me hope. Little did I know that this was just the start of a long journey filled with many challenges.

Arriving home was particularly difficult. I expected John to be proud of my success in getting out of the hospital. I thought he would be happy to see me. But he was furious with my lawyer friend and concerned that his brother-in-law, Brian, had chosen to pick me up. There were still so many unknowns.

The incident in the hospital where I threw my wedding ring at John was not the only time of anger and resentment toward him. I felt that he had violated me in a way that could have destroyed my career.

Rational thinking is hard to regain after such trauma and confusion, with all the events of the incident. The people you love the most are the targets. Understandably, it is very hard for family members to comprehend and cope with such irrational backlash.

John had tried desperately to figure out my condition and then determine how best to help me. He is a chemist by training and had begun to research all the facts surrounding my condition. He looked at everything very scientifically—not emotionally.

Eventually, he forged ahead with knowledge and insight provided by a dear friend in Maine who had experience in this field of mental illness, a person with a doctorate in psychology. She was exactly that person at that time to help John see a path forward for me, a better path than being institutionalized. They were a great team.

In sports, athletes are taught to remove the clutter. They are taught to focus on the basics without concern for outside factors. John was becoming methodical about removing the clutter and guesswork surrounding our situation. I was grateful beyond measure to my husband for his endurance. I was grateful to our dear friend for reaching out and providing key education to what was in store for our future. Later, together, we were able to search out my medical team in Bangor.

HOME AGAIN

I was thrilled to be home. Maddie had settled back into her routine and was excited for my return. She was smiling and playing and being her usual happy self. Brian and Carolyn were so supportive, but without fully understanding the complexities or implications of my illness. They felt it was time for them to return to their home in Falmouth and give our family some space to figure out what exactly was happening to me. There was a welcome quiet and peace to the house as John, Maddie and I settled down.

Our daily routine returned, and I began to take my medicine. It was a tough road for my family who became filled with worry when I refused to take my meds. Stubborn attitudes prevail through such therapy. Not many individuals are ready to accept a new substance into their body when they feel healthy. With a sickness like bipolar disorder, that doubt rises to heights where the individual can truly harm themselves. For me to finally take my meds regularly was my acknowledgment of my disease, and I felt like I had finally given in to my family and doctor, and finally trusted in their thinking. Reminders from my family were unofficial interventions. But I still had my doubts, and still thought this was a temporary condition.

Each day things improved just a little bit more. I took a two-week leave in mid-October, and my assistants ran practice. At times, I came to practice and watched. I was struck by the team's normalcy in accepting me and my new temporary sideline role. They were their usual motivated, fun selves, but I still felt shame in the pit of my stomach. I was letting them down because of events outside my control. It was overwhelming to know, at that moment, I was not well enough to run practice and take charge. I did not stay long at practices because I didn't want to be a distraction. *Me, their head coach, a distraction.* That hurt me and made me anxious about rejoining the team.

―――――――――――

At the time of my first episode, another star player, and leader in the state, had committed to Maine as a junior in high school. Her perspective as a young high-schooler, and someone watching from the outside, speaks to the authenticity of her and her family. Amy Vachon was an incredible point guard who led us to championships and the single greatest moment in the history of the program to date: Maine defeating Stanford in the first round of the NCAA tournament. Amy was the catalyst and leader. She was a poised assist-maker and scoring point guard. Her passes gave each game an excitement that made the fans clamor for more. She is currently the head coach at the University of Maine. Of course, the championships have continued under her tutelage. She is one of the most outstanding young coaches in the country today.

Amy was in the unique position of being outside the team during my first episode: she was a new recruit and still in high school. Her mind is filled with many memories of those days. Despite not being a formal member on the team, initially she was aware of many details. She knew that players had gone to the hospital to find me.

As they described it to Amy: "She is our coach, she needed us, and we were going to get her back." For Amy, there was much unknown and many questions. The players talked amongst themselves, even half-joking at times, to make sense of it all. Amy became aware of the first episode by talking with the current players. More details would come out in time. Amy continued to learn more as she joined our team officially. Incredibly, the championships followed, and she was ready to make her mark as one of the greatest players ever at Maine.

The insights Amy learned about my first episode would help her understand more clearly the events that followed a few years later.

When dealing with any team or organization, seeking truth and coming to it quickly is the best course of action. I could have helped the team significantly with more clarity from the start. But the "stigma virus" was leading my thinking. With my mental health being challenged every day, at this time especially, it would be critical to have been as clear and as forthright as possible. The challenge continues to be a great one because education is so important. How can we diagnose more quickly? How can we get the right medical parties on the same page, safely and effectively, in a timely manner? People do get sick and miss work or opportunities. How can we treat mental health sickness the same as all others that traumatize our world? How can we remove the fear? Can we save just one life by the proactive diligence of people surrounding the sick individual? Is being sick with a mental health issue different than a person being treated for cancer? Both diseases challenge the mind and body. Both can affect judgment and the ability to physically perform. Questions and more questions abound. Will we arrive at the day where the facts will be clearer, and breed more confidence in our brain health? I am so fortunate to have lived a life with so much early support, when times were less progressive, and been able to coach incredible women for so many years. The players' love and support pushed for truth and answers.

———————————

After my first appointment with "Dr. Sally," I began to buy in to the disease ever so slightly. Still I had doubts about the meds initially assigned to me, but Dr. Sally, a renown psychiatrist with a track record of great success, gave me greater confidence with each appointment. Dr. Sally, who has since retired, was simply an expert in her field, and she had a sense of humor that made me smile. She earned my trust by asking simple questions that were relaxing. Her empathy toward me and all that had happened, and her general demeanor, let me know that she was on my side. She also made me believe that I could, in fact, have another child despite my disease and issues. Her quiet confidence and even quirkiness were so refreshing. I felt calmer and convinced that I could handle any of this, that I was a fighter and I would be back better than ever.

I can remember telling Dr. Sally that I am a person who goes against the grain, and that I did not totally accept her diagnosis and questioned my original treatment plan. The first medicine I took was Depakote, immediately following the first episode. Later, and with more insight and planning and under Doctor Sally's direction, I was taking lithium.

———————————

Following my first episode, and despite my family's support, and concerns about my behavior, I still remained in denial about the scope of my illness. I simply could not accept that I, a former athlete, could have such trouble with my brain. However, with the help of my meds and counseling, I had come down off my manic high and understood that I had landed in a mental state that was still very serious and scary. The thought that I was being persecuted by my family or those individuals at the hospital was replaced with the reality of slowly accepting my mental illness. I had lost weight due to erratic eating and a lack of appetite. I had transitioned to a low mood of acceptance at this time. Still, I remained reluctant to take my medicine.

I still felt the pride of being a former student athlete. I worked out hard and continued to do so in my life. *There must be a way for me to get well without introducing into my body foreign substances that could impact my long-term health.* I wanted to get better. I was getting better each day. But, the long-term commitment of being a drug-taking lifer and a prisoner to this situation made me pause and resist.

My brother came to visit. Rich is a strong guy with good thoughts, and it was touching that he would come see me and talk to me about what was happening. We discussed many things that night. He did a great job of not asking too many questions. He was able to make small talk and not make me the center of attention. At the end of his visit he simply said, "Please take your meds. We all want you healthy, and do it for Maddie if you must. But you must do it."

Tears welled up as I thought of the people I could hurt if I did not respond to the therapies. During situations of imbalance, hurting other people is not something that the newly diagnosed consider. The diagnosed individual is at a complete loss for words and understanding. There is a saddened wonderment of how to hold on to *you*. I was trying to make sense of it all, and trying to keep my own integrity under control. I was holding on too tight. I had lost sight of what was important.

A few weeks later, it was my brother-in-law, Tom, who visited and made that point simply and with love, again. He said in a very calm way, "You can hurt the very people you are fighting to protect. Pride is important, but love and family are much more so."

Indeed, time was passing quickly. I was growing closer to understanding my own truth. Two brothers, two visits, with much wisdom to absorb.

If you are a former athlete, you especially believe that your body is sacred. Your body is strong. There were times when I felt that if I could not be myself with my normal brain, then why would I want to be on this earth? I would be an imposter. I was not suicidal, but for once, I could understand and recognize why someone would choose to take their life, to escape. I empathized with that choice. My brain now had a new level of understanding. A brave and very scary reality became evident to me.

I still could not imagine what life would be like for me with such controls in place for my mind. I began to truly realize that I was hurting those who cared and loved me. It seems strange that I wouldn't automatically understand this as a mother, wife, and a coach. But in my condition at the time, my mind didn't work right. I became solely fixed on the idea of brain balance, and it consumed me nearly every day. The fact that I was so self-absorbed still bothers me.

———————

John did such a great job of keeping Maddie happy and in her routine, while I recovered. The doctors kept saying it would take a long time for me to heal. I found that offensive. I began taking my medicine consistently. Things were getting better rather quickly. There are many different levels of this disease and others like it, so it's hard to know exactly where the sufferer is on the continuum between "well" and "sick." After my dedication to taking my medicine, I began to slowly get into my regular routine. There were still nights that I didn't sleep well, or I was agitated. John played "Pachelbel's Canon D" for me at night, trying to soothe my mind and let me slip away into a deeper sleep, if possible.

I was turning the corner, visiting more of my team's practices. I was eager to get back on the floor with my team. Many supporters and fans wondered if it would take months, or even a year, for me to return.

After fourteen days, I was back. I never really explained to the team all the details of what happened. Some things were understood intrinsically, and some things would not be understood for many years. I was aware of the stigma attached to mental illness. I was honest about having a sudden issue with sleep and care for myself. I explained to them that I had to take some time to sort through the care I needed for my long-term future. All listened intently and strived to understand. At that time, I gave them all the information they needed. Steph and Cindy both took the lead roles in moving the team forward in every way.

University administrators remained wary, and seemed not to

know what to say. Fortunately for me, I had a great deal support from family and the community. My team knew something had been wrong of course, but the kids were amazing and eager to move forward. Their inspiration was critical to my recovery. They accepted me for who I was without question, and continued to respond to my coaching.

From that time on, we were on our way to special championships. The eight years of my life at University of Maine were remarkable for a rising head coach, in several ways. My accomplishments were far beyond expectations. But the more amazing revelation came from the incredible resilience of my teams. We all learned valuable lessons while staying true to each other every step of the way.

The lessons about myself were not quite over. But at this time, I had stabilized nicely as I headed back to coaching. It turned out that I hadn't missed as much as everyone had predicted. I was back with the team, practicing for another great season. This group was a very talented team with very high goals. I was thrilled to be back and feeling quite happy and stable in my new life. Slowly but surely, I found a way to accept the circumstance through the support of my psychiatrist and, of course, my family. As we moved through the season, the team continued to have success in all ways. Success can be remarkable when teams and coaches stick by each other through the very tough stuff.

Our overall success at Maine brought on some beautiful moments while I coached in my home state. Prior to my illness, the team found a way to make a little history. On January 9, 1995, Cindy Blodgett and Steph Guidi and the entire team found a way to knock off the University of Alabama, the number-nine-ranked team coming off a Final Four appearance the prior season. We won at home in front of fifty-eight hundred screaming Black Bear fans. Cindy Blodgett had 30 points as a first-year player, and defended the star guard in the final play for them to tie the game. Their star made a move and lost her balance without getting off a decent shot at the buzzer. Game over, 75-73. Maine achieves the greatest upset in its history to date. Pure bedlam. Later, as I became a more balanced and healthier coach and in the best space ever of my career, extraordinary things happened for the team and all of those supporting the program regarding winning numerous conference championships. But it is the NCAA games that I remember most.

One of the most disappointing not-so-close games in the NCAA tournament was a sound defeat by North Carolina State University, led by a legend in the game—Kay Yow.

Earlier that year, I had endured my second manic episode, but we were well beyond that situation: we went on to win the conference again, and then take on the mighty North Carolina State University in the NCAA tournament. I thought it was strange we did not compete so well against the Wolfpack, and wondered if there were some residual effects from my second episode. Later, as Amy reminded me, the team had their own problems that year going unresolved. This was more than a freeing comment to me—this was enlightenment, as I had been worrying that the pain I had inflicted unknowingly was affecting everything, all the time.

Typically for sufferers of my disease, I began to feel like everything was my fault. If a player catches a cold, is that some kind of effect from my issues? But Amy made it clear that I was not the person who provided the situation that led that team to instability—she smiled later and said, "We had our own issues." It was refreshing to hear that from former a trusted point guard and great player. That year, NC State showed their continued dominance as they went all the way to the Final Four. Coach Yow was beyond gracious in singing the praises of our team. The late Kay Yow is truly a legend beyond measure in the women's game and far beyond. She continues to impact lives around the globe with the Kay Yow *Play for Kay Game* to support funding for breast cancer and all cancers. Her legacy is alive and well with all of us. Despite the three-point loss in the next year's NCAA Tournament at LSU, to another legend Sue Gunter and her team, the team's efforts supported the narrative that the Maine women's program could compete nationally on the big stage.

The next season, we took on Stanford in the first round of the NCAA tournament. Stanford women's basketball has always been one of the very best programs in the country. Led by Olympic coach Tara Vanderveer, they have been nothing short of sensational with their national championships and consistency. Tara's book, *Shooting from the Outside,* had just come out and I was reading it as we prepped for the game. Tara is a coach I had always followed and seen as a mentor and a superior leader and example for women's basketball, all sports, and life in general. We saw each other at the NCAA meeting prior to competition, and she noticed that I was reading her book. With her wry sense of observation she said, "Do you like the book?" I replied, "Yes, I am hoping for some kind of small edge." We both laughed. Maine won 58-56 in an incredible game, the first and only time to date that Maine has advanced in the NCAA tournament.

In the final game of NCAA play, and my last season with Maine, we took on the University of North Carolina Tar Heels, yet another great team, led by Hall of Famer Sylvia Hatchell. The NCAA Tournament schedulers had configured Maine to play UNC in Santa Barbara, California—truly a beautiful place to visit, and my team was thrilled. For me, I was happily pregnant with Jack. My due date was right around the corner as we took off for that NCAA experience. With permission from my doc, we were off for the cross-country journey. We battled UNC hard in a back-and-forth game. We lost that game by three points to end our excellent season. Again, despite the outcome, Maine was competing at the highest level. Coaching a game across the country, at nine months pregnant, proved to be an ultimate challenge.

Our overall success at Maine had been incredible. Although these four season squeakers were so very heartfelt by all of us, we kept building and growing as a program. The teams and their resolve had much to do with that impressive reality. We had won on and off the court by winning one game out of four in these NCAA tournaments. We were a top mid-major program with more stories than anyone could possibly recall. Despite the tournament game outcomes, there was a national championships spirit to those Maine women I will never forget.

GOING ROGUE

L ooking back on the details of this precarious time, I can see the insidious nature and personal challenges within mood disorder care: I decided, unbelievably, two years later in the fall of 1997, to stop taking my medicine. Although this choice seems irrational now, it seemed perfectly logical to me at the time. I was "fixed" and back as my old self. It seemed that the medicine had done its job, and I was well on my way to being medicine-free. I was eager to make a change and to get back to being the real me. Despite all we had endured in the first episode, my mind still could not accept that I was different. In this case, time had healed my thinking inappropriately: I was still looking for a way out, and I wanted to be *normal.* Perhaps the first episode had all been a mistake, or just a short blip in my life? I could not yet accept myself as a person who would take medicine forever. Despite all my education and experiences with mood disorders, I came right back to the point where I thought I knew better. I also knew that I would not tell *anyone* of my newly devised independence.

I felt I was stronger than ever. We were playing great ball and our leadership was evident in all areas. There is a common saying in sports: "If it's meant to be, it's up to we." Alas, there is a similar version that I subscribed to at this time: "If it's meant to be, it's up to *me.*" This is the spirit in which I decided to stop taking my meds. I felt it was time for *me* to stand alone, and show that I had overcome all my difficulties. I was being strong in a silent way, privately. Self-reliance and self-preservation are characteristics of any athlete or team in accomplishing goals and dreams. My secret decision had the effect of making me feel whole again, and truly in charge of my own destiny.

With lack of restful sleep, and after I stopped taking my meds in late October of 1997, my next bipolar/depressive episode actually surfaced the following February, two and a half years after my first episode. As my severe anxiety surfaced, John, along with our dear friends, Terry and Stan, drove me to our game in Boston. This was highly unusual, as I always travelled with the team on the bus. I had a dramatic sense of worry and anxiety. My concentration level was affected, and the basic coaching thoughts and strategies blurred—I could not even manage plays inside my head. What was happening to me? *It* was happening again, in a different form. This time my altered state was not filled with great knowledge and focus. Instead, I was a depressed and anxious coach with an imbalanced and struggling mind. John felt strongly that I should not coach that game. I was angry and irritable, and deeply resented being told I was unfit to coach. I fought him with every convincing word I could muster. But there I was, coaching in a game after a big change in my meds. The team battled through the chaos, but the conditions were not conducive to focus and execution. I was a distraction. We were the better team, but lost by a large margin. John later recalled, "Only later did I see and learn about how things unfolded for the team. It was a very sad time for me. I knew that you had suffered something related to the first episode. My mind was understanding, and my heart was breaking for what I saw."

Years later, as Amy shared her memories with me, guilt and shame permeated all my thoughts. I had done the unthinkable. I had gone off my meds to prove a point of independence, and the very people I loved were hurt without explanation. The season marched on with success. Of course, there were residual trust issues stemming from the first episode, wounds still healing. Again, the players were uncomfortable, but they were still ready to move on and win another championship. My actions had to speak, as I had to show them that I would be more than ready to lead. Regardless, we all galvanized together and won another tournament championship and earned the right to play in the NCAA Tournament again. The resilience, fortitude and empathy of this group drew them closer together. They would not be denied as they carried me, and the program, to great success with their incredible play, and also with their unwavering efforts to find a way to rise together. However, the players felt consequences and experiences at the time, which only came to light many years later.

Reflecting is very painful. I stayed true to my thinking and did not tell anyone that I was off my medicine. I felt well, and enjoyed my family and my coaching very much. It takes a bit of time for the mind to regroup when denied proper dosages of chemicals. Eventually that happened to me. But it was not a hypo-manic state this time; it was the opposite end of the spectrum. A sense of loss and low feelings took over my thinking, especially at night. I did not understand these feelings because they did not match the genuine success the team was having, or the distorted feelings I experienced during my first episode. I began to question my thoughts. Things became blurred, and it was exceedingly difficult to concentrate. I tried to read the newspaper in the morning, and I had to really work to focus, just to make sense of what I was reading. My eyes jumped around the page, and I was unable to comprehend or see the words clearly.

Sleep was also becoming a problem again. Anxiety lurked one night as I knew that I had an important TV interview to tape the next day with an interesting television host. A coach's responsibilities do not slow down, regardless of how she feels. I knew I had to deep breathe and stay calm, but more importantly, I knew that I had compromised my brain health just to make an personal point. I decided that it was time to come clean to John, and to our few friends who understood my condition.

But when the patient stops taking medication, there is a high degree of illness recurrence that can present in many different forms. Later, after the episode, I had enough presence of mind to consult with my doctor. Dr. Sally sat me down and we talked about the difficulty and risk of going on and off medicine. She educated me more about my condition. I was told I would be better than ever if I simply would follow her lead, allow her to help me with the medicine, along with some cognitive behavioral therapy.

Sometimes the lessons of life have to be extreme for a person to really understand the gravity of the situation. I had such an experience during that game in Boston and the team, once again, solidified my new-found commitment to my health. During this second episode, in our Boston hotel the evening before the game, I had taken an older generation mood-disorder medicine. Taking this drug created very challenging and scary consequences the next day, which was game day. Combined with my other medicines, the revised med cocktail forced my jaw to lock up and I was unable to speak. It got worse during the afternoon as we prepared for the game. I was very nervous about this occurrence, yet failed to tell anyone or even call my doctor. I thought for sure it was going to settle down by game time, but quite the opposite occurred. The game emotions and intensity did not help. My jaw grew tighter and tighter, and my tongue swelled and made conversation difficult, almost impossible. Ironically, if I had trusted my husband about the situation or told anyone like a trainer or immediate doctor, I'd have known that Benadryl would have solved my ill-timed reaction.

"I felt strongly that you should not be coaching in that game," John recalled. "The team was disorganized and completely distracted. The supportive side of me made me feel angry at the whole situation, and wondering why the team could not play through the game, and even play for you. I saw things as a chemical issue that was solvable. Then,

I could see what was happening, and there was nothing I could do, at the time, to help."

Of course, this caused great difficulty in the game as the players noticed something was wrong with me. I tried my best to coach as usual, but it was impossible. There was fear in the eyes of the players. We lost that game and I left, wondering what exactly was happening to me. The team deserved my best, which I had been delivering throughout the season—up to this point.

"Coach was sick one day and did not attend practice. I thought this was odd because she had never been sick nor missed any practices. Soon one day turned into two and then three," recalled Amy Vachon, a key point guard, who would lead us to many championship games.

"At this point, nothing more was communicated," Amy said. "The older players who had experienced the first episode two years ago, were beginning to talk and wonder if something similar was happening again. Then, Coach missed the entire week of practice.

"We had a game upcoming away in Boston. Coach did not travel with the team. The team and I thought this very weird. Shooting practice was odd as well, since coach did not engage with the team. The assistants ran the show. Weird again, as there was not precedent for coach's behavior. The locker room was up a flight of stairs. As the team ran there, I heard someone say out loud that 'something was not right.' Coach had an assistant do the pregame talk, which also was unprecedented. The locker room had a full-length mirror so the team could see everything behind us. Coach stood in the back as one of our assistants gave the pregame talk. The second time the team came back in the locker room, the other assistant gave the last key three points to the team. Also, Coach sat the entire time during the game. "All of this confusion led to our worst game of the year. We lost by thirty points to an inspired inferior team that most likely could see and recognize we were coming from a place of weakness. After the game, as the team returned to the locker room, Coach began to talk with us about the game. Her tongue was swollen, and she could not talk clearly. The team was stunned and wondering further as to what was happening. The next morning, Coach brought the entire team to her hotel room. She explained that an allergic reaction to some type of medicine caused the problems. The team accepted her explanation. Coach expressed how bad she felt, sorry that she had put us all in such an emotionally vulnerable position."

Again, the team proved to be resilient and dedicated. There was no blaming after that loss. They knew I was not well during the game, but they refused to make excuses. I had no excuses to make. I did it to myself, and then to the team. Indeed, what you do to yourself, you do to the team. I owed them my undivided focus and health. We were more fortified than ever. No excuses. Onward we charged.

My doctor was aware that I very much wanted to have more children. Maddie was already out in the world and was a happy child. Dr. Sally and I had many discussions about the reality of this, and how it could happen, given the medication I was taking at the time. During my depressive period while I tried to self-manage my medication, it turned out I had gotten pregnant. At first there was a sense of jubilation and excitement to think about John and me welcoming a second child into this world. Later, toward the end of the season, I was back to my gynecologist and my worst fears were realized.

March and early April had arrived after a very successful season. We had won the league and conference championships and competed heroically in the NCAA tournament, losing by three at LSU. Cindy was being drafted to the WNBA. It was a jubilant time for her and for the program. No player had ever been drafted to the WNBA from the University of Maine.

On the day of a press conference to discuss Cindy's success, I was returning from an ill-timed doctor's appointment and follow-up. It had been determined that the fetus, my second pregnancy, was not viable. A dilation and curettage (D&C) was performed right away. There were many tears and much sadness. But now I had to get myself ready to celebrate one of the most unique times in a student-athlete's life. I can remember my extreme mix of emotions on that day. I was able to put myself in my coaching space, and speak proudly about Cindy as one of the greatest basketball players in the country, at the press conference. I was thrilled for Cindy and her family. She was starting a very new and exciting life.

As I left the press conference, it was all I could do to get to my car. Running to the car and shutting the door with a brisk bang allowed me to be quiet, shedding many tears of fear and sadness. Letting those tears flow was the only therapy I had at the moment. I had no idea how comforting it could be to be in a car, alone, releasing every one of my mixed and complicated emotions. Quietly, silenced with my own thoughts, and having to handle myself emotionally brought a sense of peace to the agony.

After having the episodes while coaching, and the medicine complications, followed by a miscarriage, I finally grasped that it was time to figure out my new life as a bipolar person. My effort to find independence had proven tragic, and I knew I could only blame myself. Shame and regret filled my emotional world. This time I had to truly take care of me, and all those surrounding me, with a complete commitment to how much my loved ones were engaged in my new life. It would be a total team effort. It was time to step away mentally with maturity and understanding, and sort things out so I could be there for my family and for my team.

Dr. Sally proved to be an incredible person in my life. She changed my medication and put me on lithium while explaining the long-term dangers of the medicine. Despite those concerns, it seemed like the right choice for me because I was determined to have another child.

At this point, things got better at home and with my work. We found a lithium balance that seem to blend with my brain almost perfectly. John was enthusiastically on board, as it gave him some scientific relief and hope that lithium was the right fit for me.

Although it sometimes seemed like a violation of privacy, I was always checking blood levels and reporting back to my doctor. Those who take lithium must keep track of lithium levels in their body so that their doctors can monitor the dosage. Lithium is on the periodic table of elements and is a natural salt, but as a medication it must be monitored closely to get the best mind-health results. I had to search out testing sites to draw blood for the labs. I despised this process: I was a public figure and did not want to be recognized. I took lithium for the rest of my time in Maine through MSU and to Duke. But when I relocated, I lacked trust and did not have a regular doctor, so I stuck with Dr. Sally in Maine. I talked with her on the phone, and the blood levels were sent to her via the labs. I also visited her once a year to check in, to confirm that my lithium levels were safe. I was handling my responsibilities for years, and it felt good.

In order to try and stay anonymous when getting blood drawn, I went to different clinics to get my levels checked. Slowly, I adapted in getting a routine in my new life, taking medicine, checking my blood levels, and being grateful that my doctor would continue to work with me. The motivator was simple: if I was on lithium, I could have another child. My life took on a wonderful cadence, and the team continued to win championships together.

We made another trip to the NCAA tournament in March 2000 as I was on my way to understanding more about myself. My eight years at Maine had been remarkable in so many ways. And for the most part, my privacy was protected. Most people knew I had endured issues surrounding my pregnancy at Maine, and there was certainly speculation. But, I felt my bipolar self was basically private and left alone. Mainers are respectful and loyal people. No

one ever asked about that personal time. At a Maine football game,
I remember seeing one of the male nurses who had held me down in
the hospital years earlier. He called my name to say "Hello." I looked
at him with skeptical and discerning eyes, initially unsure of who he
was. The entire hospital experience was still surreal and tucked away
in my past. I had forgiven, but it was clear that I would never forget.
What remained at the top of mind for decades were the players at
Maine who supported and rallied around me during my darkest
times. Many have become lifelong friends.

Throughout my ordeal, my Maine players were incredibly brave
and inquisitive. I now realize that those special women kept me
in coaching and gave my life and my family so many incredible
experiences. Young people have an incredible resilience that
motivates me daily. The student-athletes can rise in ways that are
simply awe-inspiring.

The championship team mentality began with special individuals
who cared enough to keep their team and their head coach together,
no matter what the cost or challenge. They were in the midst of
the battle, not by choice, but by chance and circumstance. They
personified the courage and bravery it took to move forward in a
world of conjecture and uncertainty. To succeed, and even flourish,
in the face of this uncertainty is a remarkable accomplishment that
many may not achieve in a lifetime.

Toward the end of my career at the University of Maine, John and
I became pregnant again. This time we had to monitor the pregnancy
closely. My doctors were superlative. There was a small chance of
heart complications when a fetus is exposed to lithium *in utero*. I
worked closely with my doctors to accept the risks, while getting
past the guilt of ingesting a medicine that could potentially harm my
baby. Despite the traumatic experiences of my past, I knew that my
medicine was critical. Going off any meds at this point would risk

doing more harm to the baby than my taking lithium daily. My logical brain could understand this, but my emotional brain had a hard time reconciling the risk involved to helping shape my son's heart.

Naturally, as parents we had to wander faithfully through the pregnancy and hope everything would be okay. There were many days of tears and concern. There were many appointments to monitor the growth of the valves in the baby's heart. Seeing a healthy heart beating during the pregnancy was one of the most beautiful pictures we would ever see in our lifetime.

With Maddie, we had allowed ourselves the secrecy of not knowing the baby's gender. With Jack, there were so many ultrasounds that we knew he was a boy. This was a thrilling time for us, and also an amazingly transitional time as well. John and I had discussed the possibility of moving, if the right circumstances presented themselves. We still loved Maine but were open to new challenges and a fresh start.

Michigan State did a great job recruiting me and my family. They kept in touch as closely as they could relative to my work at Maine. There were phone calls from Tom Izzo and from Michigan's governor. In the second half of the 2000 season, they had come to see me coach at a game in Boston, ironically, against Northeastern. We won that game on a full-court game-winning layup by Amy Vachon. On March 28, 2000, I had told the team, staff and administrators that we would be moving to Michigan to coach. It was such an emotional and difficult day. Then John Wyatt McCallie graced us with his presence after all the emotions of that day at 7:47 pm.

After eight years at the University of Maine, John and I knew we were open to a fresh start with new challenges. John was very supportive and excited. John is an adventurer who has climbed Mt. Kilimanjaro. He is always ready for the next thing. He taught at Maine, but was eager to see what he could do at MSU and the greater Lansing area.

Leaving Maine meant leaving behind players, which was one of the most vexing aspects of my decision. As I have repeatedly said, ours was a special team—like family. And among that inner circle was Lacey Stone.

Leaving Lacey and all her teammates and recruits was an ultimate emotional challenge. Lacey was highly competitive. She was a terrific player off the bench, and was part of our Maine team that beat Stanford in the first round of the NCAA Tournament. She could be very intense. Her brilliant enthusiasm could also be met with resistance as she is a high-energy person with great ideas and creative thoughts. Lacey could intimidate with her strength and personality. We did not talk directly about her personal life too closely, but one evening, on the bus ride home after a successful game, we shared a quiet moment.

Lacey is a kindred spirit to me. Bringing out the best in Lacey, and others like her, gave me great joy and purpose. Lacey came to Maine after my health episodes were past and I was well on my way to great brain balance. I was a better coach by far, able to provide players like Lacey with patience, encouragement and some discipline, too. Her eyes were just brilliant. She was always eager, and I loved coaching her.

After my family departed to MSU, Lacey returned to the Maine team to finish the season, but she would end her college career after that. Lacey confided that she would have remained on the team had I continued as its coach. I thought about her often and was sad to learn that she eventually chose not to play.

Lacey had defined her life through her commitment to her sport. She was dedicated and dared to leave Wisconsin to grow her life and game at Maine. I knew her well, and I knew that helping balance her temperament and intensity was a key to her success.

Such clarity was a result of my balance and wellness. I was better able to understand and help players like Lacey. Being balanced mentally had made me a better coach. The team made history, with

Lacey as a big part of the chemistry and enthusiasm. She taught me a great deal about balanced coaching. She is a phenomenally successful life coach and trainer now. She has taken her passion and enthusiasm to the highest level. She is sought by many different training organizations, and she runs her own successful business. She was a winner with me, and she is a winner in life. The off-court learning has been a big part of her incredible success.

"What I learned with my great coaches, and also because of my not-so-great ones, was that the court mirrors life and vice versa," Lacey aptly stated.

So true.

I would be challenged again at MSU with more player development and player off-court issues. I had no idea, with my balanced mind and coaching experience derived from the difficult experiences in Maine, how far coaching could take me and my teams.

SAND SPACE

Jack was born on March 28, 2020, in Bangor, Maine, right down the hall from where his older sister was born at Eastern Maine Medical Center. It was the same day we announced our move to MSU. Jack was eight pounds nine ounces and even a bit early. His arrival was a welcome relief and came after we had just competed in the NCAA Tournament all the way to our last round at Santa Barbara.

It was a battle during the delivery, and we were almost headed to an emergency C-section. I was grateful to the Maine nurse who was so motivational and adamant about getting him out urgently. She was very clear.

"Joanne, you get him out NOW!" were her exact words. As she said, it was my last chance before "heading upstairs" for a C-section. Jack came out quietly, and not fully conscious. The nurse said that he had been traumatized by getting stuck in the birth canal. Regardless of her comment, I immediately thought that the lithium might have damaged him in some way during delivery. Perhaps the lithium in my system had weakened him. I was very worried as they took him away to "work on him." I looked at John and he kept his cool, reassuring me that all would be okay.

Given the dearth of research available at the time about the long-term effects of daily lithium dosages taken by a woman carrying a growing fetus, John and I were understandably anxious about

Jack's health. The pregnancy felt a lot longer as each day passed, and I dutifully had to take my meds, wondering how much I could be affecting my unborn son. We were always anxious about the ultrasound and the pictures of Jack as he developed. At each visit we felt a bit of new confidence: Jack's heart was developing normally, and the risk of complications for poor heart valve development did not seem to be occurring. Our son was growing at a rapid rate and developing as he should. We were beyond thrilled, of course. To this day there is a huge sense of wonderment about what went on inside Jack's body. What chemicals were swirling about, and how did his brain chemistry come together?

After the birth, there were some anxious moments and a significant wait, but eventually Jack was placed in my arms. We had done it! It was not the easy way, but all had worked out. We were blessed and beyond happy.

Later, when it came time to nurse Jack, I was again reminded about my condition. And this time it directly affected another human being—my baby boy. I believed strongly in nursing a baby as long as possible. I wanted to give Jack the same chances as Maddie who had benefited from such care and love five years earlier. But the nurse was clear: "You cannot nurse this baby." She explained that the risks outweighed the benefits. I was devastated. I had suspected this would be a problem, but I was eager to ignore such thoughts and nurse him anyway. The emotional connection was so important to me. I felt guilt and shame that I could not be a normal mom and give Jack my best.

Happily, things are a bit different now. A study conducted by the Massachusetts General Hospital and Harvard Medical School indicates that the lithium levels in the babies studied were at 25 percent of maternal levels. The critical piece is that there is low incidence of serious side effects in the babies exposed to lithium through breast milk. Women giving birth now have a choice if they feel the benefits of nursing outweigh the risks. Science has given women more options. The study stated clearly that infants are vulnerable to the same side effects as adults. Changes in thyroid and renal functioning are real. Clinical monitoring of lithium levels in the baby is highly recommended, and lithium levels can be tracked very closely. If today's research had been available when I gave birth, I would have nursed Jack without hesitation. I admire the science and applaud that women have choices in how they care for their babies today. Jack was a healthy baby boy. The pregnancy had been complicated and scary at times, but we made it through together, helped by having great medical care.

———————

Life was exciting as we prepared to leave our beloved Maine team and our incredible experiences.

Before exiting Orono, I returned to see the most wonderful acupuncturist I have ever encountered. Mary Margaret, with her unique and bright blue eyes and gray hair, is a stunning person, radiating with energy. She truly looked like Mother Nature. I had been seeing her for some time as she had helped me cope with recovering from my earlier miscarriage. I will always remember what she said upon my departure. When she asked where I was moving, and I replied "Michigan," she had a wonderful, broad, and beautiful smile, and made a deep sigh. She looked at me and said that Michigan is perfect.

"Why is it so perfect for me?" I asked.

Mary Margaret said, "Oh, Joanne, don't you know that Maine is a granite state? It's made of rock and it often doesn't change much without great force. It is hard to change people, as Mainers can be set in their ways. You, my dear, are a firestarter. Rock can put out fire. You need a different kind of place that offers more freedom and movement of energy."

Of course, she had me captivated by this explanation of how we might respond to life in Michigan. She then asked me directly,

"What is Michigan made of?" I said I wasn't sure what she meant. Her reply," Michigan is made of sand and surrounded by water. It's a more flowing place in the Midwest. It's a different kind of experience you will have for your peace of mind." And then, with her gracious smile and deep blue eyes she said, "I think you will have some of the best times of your life there." That was my very last meeting with Mary Margaret. I will always remember her, and those therapeutic predictions. She was correct.

———————————

The move to East Lansing was very exciting for the entire family. We inherited a program that the school administration clearly expected to rise to the top. This was the "big leagues" of college basketball, the elite and highly competitive Big Ten Conference, where expectations were high and media coverage intense. In seven years, The MSU Women Spartans would develop fast: from no postseason play, up to the Final Four of the WNIT tournament, and then all the way to the NCAA Final Four and national championship game in 2005.

Home life was blissful as well. Our kids were extremely happy in their schools and community. John was in the classroom again, teaching economics at MSU. This stability at home allowed me to toil happily as the head coach of women's basketball, to build the program I and the administration had hoped for.

Through it all, I maintained a life with lithium. I was on a regular dosage and kept in contact with Dr. Sally in Bangor. She requested that I see her at least once a year, and that I get all my blood work done on a regular basis. I always looked forward to my summer trips back to Maine. Every visit I would drive north and visit with Dr. Sally in person.

Privacy has always been a huge concern for me and my off-court world.

I never looked to find another psychiatrist or physician to take over my case in East Lansing. My mind was in a great place for the entire seven years and there were no issues, problems or any complications. I felt connected and safe with Dr. Sally. She had led me, through teaching me to take my medicine, changing my medicine, and allowing for me to have a baby boy while taking lithium every day.

The highlight of my basketball career at MSU was, of course, participating in the national championship game, which happened before I turned forty.

———————————

My experience at Michigan State is almost a blur. In five years, we went from the bottom of the Big Ten to playing for a national title. Our staff was terrific. Three key people dominated the in-state recruiting: Felisha Legette-Jack, now a very successful head coach at Buffalo; Katie Abrahamson, now a very successful coach at Central Florida; and Janelle Burgess (a former head coach at Grand Valley State). These women helped build a special team with Michigan players. They added a very special center from Papillion Nebraska, Kelli Roehrig, and a super-quick guard from Ohio in Rene Haynes, currently the head coach at Long Island University.

Our Michigan State team competed successfully against some of the top Big Ten programs almost right away. We beat a top-ten team in Georgia on CBS sports at home in a dominant game. I was able to be a part of carrying the winter Olympic torch through a part of East Lansing, and on the same weekend, both men's and women's programs at MSU moved into an incredible new facility. Another time, I met Larry Bird and Ervin "Magic" Johnson on the day of an alumni game for the guys, and many former Spartans had come back. Larry had agreed to coach against Magic. Fun times, no doubt, since they were both iconic figures to me.

Interestingly, Larry came to my practice unannounced. I was not quite sure if the very tall person with blond wavy hair was actually him. He had brought his daughter to see our team. Of course, the team had been taught to always focus and be immune to anyone who visited practice. So the team kept practicing and I kept wondering. . . but not really wondering. Larry Bird came over and very politely introduced himself and his daughter, and I tried to keep my cool. Finally, I broke our team focus with a smile, and everyone came over to meet this famous ballplayer and his lovely, inquisitive daughter.

All our hard work paid off in 2005. We won the Big Ten regular season title and the Big Ten tournament title and found ourselves a NCAA tournament number one seed for the first time in MSU history. We battled through the NCAA tourney, defeating some great teams like USC, Vanderbilt, Stanford, and Tennessee before bowing out to Baylor in the NCAA title game. ESPN gave us a lot of love as we were underdogs in the minds of all media. We thought we were pretty good: unranked to start the season, finishing second in the national polls. We maintained our fighter mentality like fearless warriors who could never be intimidated.

———

In 2005, I was voted Associated Press Coach of the Year. Al Brown, Anne Marie Gilbert and Semeka Randall were all new assistants that year and kept us in the right mindset. Al Brown brought years of coaching experience, after having worked with Pat Summit at Tennessee for multiple national championships, and his impact was unique and special. Katie Abrahamson, Felisha Legette-Jack and Janel Grimm laid the foundation for our success with their great recruiting. All the coaches were key to the team's growth and development. Nate Lake, our director of basketball operations, and his wife, Pat, were huge influences on that team as well, offering wisdom and special occasional meals that developed chemistry every step of the way.

The ESPN interviews and attention to the underdog team in the Final Four was a lot of fun. At age thirty-nine, I was the youngest coach to serve in that Final Four. I was selected Big Ten Coach of the Year, Nike Coach of the Year, and AP National Coach of the Year was a real tribute to our team's amazing 33-4 record, with wins at UConn, at Notre Dame, vs. Vanderbilt, Stanford and Tennessee in the NCAA Tournament.

As I walked off the court in Indianapolis on the evening after the NCAA semifinal-round victory versus vaunted Tennessee, I had such a feeling of joy and pride in our team and program. I looked up to the heavens and said, "Please don't let this be it." I, like a true coach, was thinking ahead and wondering if I would ever return to this grand stage with another team.

My IQ and overall coaching skills improved enormously from my time at Maine. While in my first year at MSU, I met one of the most unique individuals of my career: Dr. Lonny Rosen is a professor of psychiatry and worked directly with the athletic department at MSU for more than forty years. No person, outside of the team members themselves and immediate staff, contributed more to our success at MSU than Dr. Rosen as he became a mentor, confidant, and guiding force in my coaching life for the next twenty years.

I was not familiar with the field of sports psychiatry until joining MSU. I befriended Dr. Rosen, who had specialized in sports psychiatry and worked directly with the student-athletes. His résumé and clientele were impressive. He was a renowned football consultant assisting in multiple national titles and consulting with other programs nationwide, and others approach him routinely. I would come to admire how Dr. Rosen kept his work private and behind the scenes. He would never talk to media or share any details about his work.

Our collegial relationship began my first year at MSU, on the day he stopped by my office to introduce himself. I was apprehensive to think I was coaching at a level that required sports psychiatry. Many coaches were leery of general psychobabble used with student-athletes. Some believed the approach confused student-athletes or interfered with a coach's plan for a particular player. Enormous trust must be present for this kind of partnership to thrive. But immediately I was taken with the soft-spoken erudite man who clearly explained his role at MSU. He knew some valuable history and shared insights of the program and of MSU. We met briefly, and I was very intrigued.

Later, I learned of his awesome professional capacity as he worked closely with so many top coaches. I began to call him "Lonny," as he preferred, and I listened. There were numerous issues with my new group at MSU. Trust issues were combined with identity issues, and doubts about how good we could be were very evident, so year one for me was a lesson in patience and perseverance. I quickly began to understand how his work would weave methodically through my actions. He addressed the athletes only one-on-one. He was not a fan or believer in addressing the team as a group. He was a meticulous and patient man who loves the student-athletes and sports in general.

When my world was stressed by a young person's doubt or confusion, Lonny was always a phone call away to offer guidance. Nothing was too high-pressure for him. He also brought a Philadelphia street-smart sense of life and humor to the table. He took time to evaluate my thinking and supply his measured advice appropriately.

There were many discussions about how to move forward with the "alpha dog" characters on the team, those who prefer to lead and speak up regularly. Then, there are the quiet "assassins" who have a certain focus and deviousness in their eyes. A team with a balance of both types of competitors can be extremely effective because all the players are highly competitive and welcome the pressure. They often are the ones who come up with the game winning moves and plays.

Lonny helped me truly see the personalities of the team members, and respond to their concerns promptly with a clear understanding of their situation. The advice was never trite and packaged. Every situation was examined uniquely. As a rookie Big Ten coach, I was cutting the learning curve tremendously with this newfound resource and relationship.

His one-on-one meetings were most effective. He avoided labels and kept it simple. And his advice was pragmatic. I remember how he helped me deal with those student-athletes who were obsessed with making mistakes.

"Catch her doing things right," he would suggest. "Be very specific to her directly. Correct. Compliment. Reassure, and move away from outcomes."

With another player, who was very strong-willed and clearly an emerging leader, truly an "alpha" in personality, words were the key. "Remind her that if she sees anything that is not good for the team, say it. Speak up and lead by your voice and observation of what is best for the team."

This student-athlete wanted tough and direct coaching with no inferences attached to the comments. She had grown up with over-supportive parents who made assumptions, and asserted that she did not listen to them. I was very technical and direct with her. I loved coaching her hard, just as she had requested in our meetings. This kind of direct coaching was what she expected. Her alpha character was evident as she enjoyed being pushed beyond her own vision of herself as a player.

Another player chose to lead by example. The coach-player relationship was important to her. She had a true knack for the game. Again, sticking with technical coaching and allowing her to lead by example proved a good strategy. Another player would freeze up and withdraw in a crowd. She also did not trust herself to say the right thing to her teammates in challenging situations. She melted when faced with authority. Coaching her to compete only with herself was key to her growth. In social settings we encouraged her to smile, to be her authentic self and to find her own words with her teammates and coaches. Rewarding her when she did things right and expressed herself verbally was the key.

All information shared with Dr. Rosen was confidential. Each student-athlete was given the choice to work with him or not. The majority of my players relished the idea of performance enhancement with these meetings. Given his strict adherence to confidentiality, Dr. Rosen could only direct my thinking with each student-athlete. He provided a sort of map of how to best motivate each individual.

One of my favorite discussions with Lonny was about the concept of frontrunners. These are teams that thrive on their leading players and rely on the them to dominate games. They are also the teams that establish a point lead, get comfortable, and relax. A team like this can be up twenty and look like the greatest team ever. But if there is strong resistance by the opponent, the frontrunner team can lose its poise. Sometimes there are simply key plays that reverse the momentum and create the outcome doubt for that frontrunning team. They then cannot be as relaxed, given the changing scenario.

Then, close games get a little bit closer, and the underdog is now on the chase to knock off the frontrunning team. Oh, how we love these games, particularly in the NCAA tournaments! Those top teams that are vulnerable in this way can beat opponents over and over again by twenty, thirty and even forty points. But when a game is close, and time and score situations arise, they revert back to their uncomfortable mechanical executions, often with failure following. You can see it in their eyes and with their body language. Shots that went in easily before are now missed. Rushed shots are taken as the frontrunner team tries to get comfortable in its new role. The frontrunner team gets spooked and the proverbial "choke" is in motion. The aggressive, perhaps under-respected team, comes back and does the unthinkable, and there you have an upset. Great teams can be frontrunners or comeback warriors. They can play and succeed in every game. They can play both roles and are resilient and impervious to the opponent. They always compete amongst themselves without regard to the other team's position in the game.

The language of team sports is fascinating. A great mentor can put everything into a context individually and to the team, as Lonny had done for us countless times. The head coach observes, listens to counsel, and coaches each player individually. All the teachings and proper focus are applied throughout the season. In our case at MSU, it was one of those special comeback games Lonny and I had discussed that put us on the stage for the championship game.

I often joked that I am a perfect combination to be a coach, being a British-Italian and thus an interesting blend of uprightness and passion. There were always interesting sidebar comments. Lonny and I had a well-formed and enjoyable professional partnership. There were also his laser-sharp diagnoses.

One of the biggest breakthroughs came during the sophomore year of Kristin Haynie. Kristin was an incredible talent. She had the potential to be one of the best guards in the country. But Kristin was often sick and contracted mononucleosis the summer after her first year. As a true point guard, her role was absolutely pivotal to the team's success.

Physicians were having a tough time assessing Kristin's health situation. One day Kristin went to see Lonny. After a discussion about her childhood, and about the polyps that were removed from her intestine at a young age, her life and ours began to change. Lonny figured out that Kristin's body did not absorb nutrition properly. She would need approximately four thousand calories per day to keep up her strength and energy as a top Division I athlete. The average adult woman expends about half that amount.

After meeting with Dr. Rosen and receiving his recommendation, an MSU dietician was able to work with Kristin daily. Finally, Kristin was on her way her way to great health and leading our team to heights never experienced before at MSU.

The growth of the team throughout that year 2004-2005 was remarkable. Again and amazingly, we beat Stanford, Connecticut, Notre Dame and Tennessee in the same season. We started the season unranked and finished number two behind Baylor in the final poll rankings.

———

Lonny's deep dark eyes, thoughtful, appraising manner, and quiet direct delivery, exuded calm and generated ideas that help orchestrate the themes and focus for success. I would learn that he does not call coaches. Coaches must establish a relationship and call him. He stays in his lane and refuses to over-step his ground. He has no interest in media or any of the hype that is involved with high-level athletics.

I was the only female coach to work with Dr. Rosen and coach in a national championship game. I felt a part of the "boys' club" as he worked meticulously with so many football teams. I loved the gender-equity component, which was a quiet barrier to break to provide further opportunities for my teams. I had never seen such an immediate positive reaction from young people under his tutelage. I was thrilled to have him as a partner in competition throughout my seven years at MSU and, later, for twelve years at Duke. He provided that "safe zone" that is so rare in the field of coaching. Rational right thinking over guesswork and emotion. He is the classic reason-over-emotion mentor. With the many ups and downs of the coaching world, he proved to be a respite for all.

I wish all coaches, at all levels, could find "that person" who can help guide the delicate thinking of sports psychiatry, and its role for high-performing athletes for their programs. There is no doubt that my personal background with mental health issues provided an understanding and pathway to learning and trusting the uniqueness of such mental preparation and support.

Among the many observations he made over our time working together, two that Lonny shared with me made an enormous difference in my coaching and personal life. The first highlights the value of effective leadership in a challenging Final Four situation. The second pertains to a mental health conversation, and the power of words, and delivery, in mental health communication.

This nugget, given at a critical time of post-healing for me, ten years after my diagnosis, set the tone for my personal growth, and comfort with the realities of my life. The freeing words Lonny used changed my perspective almost immediately.

These two thoughts he shared after our Tennessee victory, and later in the spring that year, were very provocative, helpful, and never to be forgotten, and they were shared again, at a later time in our relationship. One applied to the court, while the other was more personal in nature. Simple words and wisdom were carefully presented to allow me to coach, and be free within my own professional and personal world.

––––––––––––––––

Looking back to my most exciting time at Michigan State, all MSU folks were positively stunned after a thrilling comeback win over Tennessee in the 2005 National Semi-Final. MSU women's basketball took center stage at a school defined by Coach Izzo and men's basketball history and success. We took over the game at the nine-minute mark where we were down sixteen, and we never looked back as we forged the greatest single comeback in NCAA semi-Final Four history. We beat an enormously talented team coached by Pat Summit, who had built Tennessee into one of the elite programs in the country, on the grandest stage of them all.

Pat was the greatest coach of all time. She was a mentor to many throughout the profession of coaching. She broke all gender barriers when it came to success and respect. I had some experience coaching against her while I was a graduate assistant and assistant coach at Auburn. Pat served as a reference for my first coaching job application to the University of Maine. My in-laws were Tennesseans, and my father-in-law always reminded me that the only way to be special in the profession was to beat "The Queen." He used that description as an ultimate compliment to Coach Summit: she rose to the highest level, and brought many people along with her.

On the evening of that 2005 game my father-in-law, T. Hooke McCallie, was being cared for by the nurses in his retirement home. His health was suffering. Later in May he passed. Afterward, when I went to visit the nurses at the retirement home, one of them gently pulled me aside. She wanted to tell me that Dad had watched the Tennessee game and hung in there—despite his health—throughout the game with great pride and joy. He became ill and could not watch the National Championship game. "I believe your father-in-law passed believing you won the national championship that evening against Coach Summit," she said. I was so happy to have this thought shared with me. I just smiled broadly at the notion that Dad had celebrated my greatest victory with the best possible thoughts, prior to departing this world.

There was so much excitement in the air. Tears of joy and laughter were everywhere. Our fans were incredible as we played in front of a record crowd at the RCA Dome. I knew I had to settle in for the national title battle against Baylor.

Calling Lonny had become a welcome habit to help me articulate my post-game thoughts. Calmly, as usual, he reiterated a concept that we had previously discussed—the concept of a "relief" win. It's the idea that a team uses its maximum energies and abilities to come from behind aggressively and win, which is what occurred in our victory over Tennessee. Lonny knew we had only played seven players each game the whole season, so those players were physically fatigued, and their recovery was a huge concern. The inevitable media attention kept our players up until the early hours of the morning, and the team adrenalin was at an all-time high, leaving little time for emotional rest. With the 2005 national championship game just forty-eight hours away, I was concerned about their recovery.

Lonny was thrilled for our success. As a person with a great sense of game realities and experiences for years, he was always getting the coach to think ahead. Gently, and with pure honesty, he reminded me that getting the team to move on would be the hardest game prep. We had burned too much fuel against Tennessee, and there was not a lot a coach could do at this point except be aware and try to drive the team through the victorious history-making fog.

In coaching, we are always working against some element of human nature. In sport, as a coach, you are always finding a way to sort through how to will your team to think from a higher space. Within the battlegrounds of film and game prep, some coaches can miss the real issues if they are not in tune with the pulse and emotional pace of a team.

We prepared for Baylor as best we could. During the game I stayed calm and we battled and gave everything we had, but found ourselves overcome by a hot Baylor team.

The words and wisdom Lonny shared prior to the game helped me prepare for that weekend. Lonny's forthright nature, while not holding back the ultimate challenge of the situation, was direct and appreciated. I wanted him to tell me that our great team would just ride the wave right through the last game. But through years of working together, I knew better. I had to hear his honest thoughts before I could move forward and get ready for all that accompanies making history, as our team had so definitively done.

Lonny's wisdom again helped me cope and find perspective a month later, after all the autographs had been signed, the banquet was over, and life had returned to a normal pace.

Spring had sprung in East Lansing and I had a special gift for my friend. I asked Lonny if I could bring that special something to his home. I maneuvered a beautiful Final Four chair into his house to say "thank you." Final Four chairs are given only to the direct participants after the event. Each one is treasured as a special piece of memorabilia. This was the most meaningful way I could think of to thank him for his total commitment to our team. We were the only women's team he had consulted that had made it to a national title game. We were the first ever women's team to play for a national title at MSU. He and I sat on his back deck, reliving the moments of that famous six-game run. The sun was shining brightly, and the temperature was comfortable. We drifted from subject to subject. It was a memorable and well-earned visit.

An incredible sense of peace came over me. I felt so comfortable and free in that moment. I began to share my story of how I had come to MSU. The details of my life regarding being bipolar, and regulating my brain with lithium, felt so easy and natural to share. He was quiet. He listened as I told more of the story, including the hospital incident. There was a comfortable silence that rested on the deck with us. I will never forget his first four words:

"It's not your fault." I was stunned. No one had ever addressed my shame in such a simple and direct way. I was speechless. I wondered for a moment if I had said too much. Then, that learned insecurity and panic for privacy drifted away with the subtle breeze on the deck. These words were some of the most valuable words he shared with me from that season.

HIGHER EXPECTATIONS

After our Final Four success, many opportunities developed. Nike was rewarding Final Four men and women coaches with wonderful trips to beautiful places. It was the first of many special trips on which we were invited. John accompanied me to Whistler, British Columbia for our very first Nike trip.

I have enjoyed a twenty-seven-year relationship with Nike. The Nike family is real. The unforgettable leadership and connection for men's and women's coaches that Nike has supported, sponsored, and generated for years is not generally known. The generosity and coaching development that is so supported by Nike is unique. The Final Four coaches's trip proved inspirational.

Most memorably, I had the chance to sit and talk with University of North Carolina Head Coach Dean Smith. Coach Smith was drawn to us by the fact that John's older brother, Wyatt, had been a Morehead scholar at UNC. This pleased him greatly. We also talked about my team and the Final Four run. He admitted sheepishly that we were his favorite women's team that year. I was honored and amazed by this statement. I certainly had some serious residual sadness from that memorable run. I knew a special chance had come for us. I knew how incredible the team was, and that teams like that are rare. I was grateful, but wondered if and when I would take another team to the Final Four. Coach Smith reached out with some poignant words.

"Your first Final Four, and you were playing for the National Championship. *Hmmm*, that puts you ahead of me."

Those were his memorable words. Coach Smith was saying that in his first Final Four, he only made it to the semi-final game before losing. My first time there as a head coach I had made it all the way to the national title game. Therefore, he said, "That puts you ahead of me," with a very humble tone and twinkle in his eye. It was this humble comment of empathy that led to a heartfelt pause for me.

He told the story of his first team to go to the Final Four, and how the semi-final game proved to be their ultimate challenge that year. I will never forget our exchange on a mountaintop, after we all paraded up the gondolas for dinner.

Basketball remained a critical part of our lives that summer as I was still in the afterglow of reaching the Final Four. I did some color commentary for the Detroit Shock of the WNBA that summer. The Shock were based in Detroit and ended up winning a world championship. I was so proud to own a world championship ring. The Shock organization was very gracious and gave rings to all who were a part of the team. Because I spent a lot of time interviewing the players on the playing floor, it was a great feeling to know that I would get a ring, too. The Shock players, coaches, and entire organization were a great group of highly motivated professionals that included Katie Smith, Deanna Nolan and Swin Cash. That opportunity followed the summer after our Final Four run. I stepped away in 2008 when the Shock demands started encroaching on my family time and recruiting, because the WNBA played in the summer months from June through to September.

━━━━━━━━

After seven seasons, my contract with Michigan State was being negotiated. During that time, I had amassed a record of 316-148 at MSU, taken us to post-season play, and we were on the precipice of winning a national championship. I had tremendous support from within MSU and its fans.

After much consideration for our family and team, John and I decided to remain open to leaving MSU if the right position presented itself. There were a few jobs of interest to us, one at Duke and the other at the University of North Carolina, *if* they ever opened.

Leaving MSU was a very difficult decision. Each year's team had been tremendously fun to coach, and we all had made history together over a short seven-year period. After my final season, we had some salary and budget negotiations with MSU, but it really was Duke's recruitment and its location that lured us most. Duke is near Chattanooga where John's family is from, plus it was a great challenge to take over a top program and see if we could take that next step to the first women's national title at Duke. My two previous experiences had been more "rebuilding" the programs. Great next step. Ultimate challenge.

I had been recruited to play for Duke when I was just a freshman in high school, choosing instead to discover Northwestern in the midwest. But I was always open to returning as the coach, to come full circle in my career, if the opportunity arose. It appeared it might be time to accept a new challenge in the beautiful city of Durham.

We had been contacted by Duke, and began to realize it would be another adventure in another part of the country. John's family was a priority and we thought it might be a good idea to get a bit closer as many of his relatives were aging. Of course, we were attracted by Duke very much, with its history of terrific basketball success. Duke presented a true powerhouse program, both academically and athletically. For me, it would be a chance to be challenged at the highest level.

———

The first year at Duke was an amazing experience of change and growth and excitement. Our family had to move during the summer as I coached the USA team in the world championships in Moscow. I had been fortunate to be selected by USA Basketball to coach first in the Americas championships in Mexico City in the summer of 2006, and then follow up with almost the same team to compete in World in Moscow the next summer. These competitions, along with the Pan American games, are lead-ups to developing talent to eventually play for the USA Olympic team. Both gold medals were very prestigious and those experiences are highlights of my career.

Maddie had a very tough time with the move to North Carolina because she was thirteen and left behind a great deal of support back in East Lansing. Jack was a bit too young to care as much— he was just an excited little boy, ready for the next adventure. But for Maddie it was a long summer, so I chose for her to accompany me and the USA team to train in France, and then to Moscow to compete. Sharing the experience with my daughter of winning the gold medal was a big highlight to that summer.

———

Duke fans are among the most ardent and dedicated in NCAA sports. And for me, that meant lots of eyes watching and evaluating. I welcomed this atmosphere and found it to be enormously stimulating. I had very big shoes to fill, and everyone was watching.

Replacing a Duke legend in Gail Goestenkors was a great challenge, after she had left Duke to take the head coaching job at the University of Texas. A head coach's sudden departure is rarely easy. I had been a part of such emotional transitions twice, and the rawness of emotions was the same at Duke. People were hurt. The team felt abandoned, and there was a hesitancy to welcome the new coach and staff. Clearly, this was a part of the game that required taking over coaching at the highest level. There is a steady truth to coaching: players want you to earn their loyalty, and coaches deliver loyalty in return. If the team wins, it is generally because of the players' execution and performance. If the team loses, it is the coach and poor decisions that receive blame. Of course, the ideal thinking is that we are all responsible together, for every game, regardless of outcome. However, the more realistic and polarized view can be pronounced at Duke and at the other schools in the basketball mecca of the famed Triangle which includes Duke, the University of North Carolina and North Carolina State. Coaches accept this reality, and we are paid well to assume the risks of the job, and to march on through all adversity and criticism.

My team and I would rise to the challenge and experience great moments at Duke with incredibly special teams. Our highlights included ACC championships and the post-season NCAA tournament successes that included going to four straight Elite Eights and numerous Sweet Sixteen appearances. The ultimate goal was to advance to the Final Four and bring a women's national championship to Duke. We were focused and preparing daily for this exciting opportunity.

The first taste I got of being under the magnifying glass at Duke came during our first year when John was reading through some blog action, which is never a good idea and can often be negative. A blog filled with sports and coaching opinions revealed that I took lithium. I was struck by this disclosure by an unnamed person, and saddened by someone's willingness to invade my private space so easily and publicly. I have no idea what that person intended, but it revealed the desperate nature of some fans to interject doubt and hearsay for me as the new coach. It was a complete violation of my privacy. My husband was furious, and we began to wonder about what kind of person would go to that degree to intrude on a coach's life. Soon afterward, the post was deleted.

I had tried to keep my personal medical condition private. My condition was balanced and steady, and I was focused, productive and able to handle the pressures of the job. Eventually, my longtime Maine doctor felt it was important for me to find a doctor in Durham to provide local support, because she was preparing to retire. She helped me alleviate privacy concerns by helping me choose a private practice outside of hospital care. I followed her advice.

I knew that being a public figure can be very risky. Everyone wants a piece of the coach. As a strong woman in a male-dominated world, I needed a tight and talented support network to help me navigate this rough-and-tumble world. At Dr. Sally's suggestion, I had met with a private counselor who paved the way for me to meet the doctor who would work with me directly. I am so grateful to her to this day. One of the amazing things she did for me was to connect me with a doctor in Chapel Hill who was not connected to any university.

Dr. P was amazing from the start. She understood my situation and collected all the data as Dr. Sally continued to work with me.

Through experience and the advice of Dr. Sally, I learned the value of working with a private practice doctor. The timing of my move from Dr. Sally to Dr. P proved to be critical.

Dr. P took a team approach to caring for me, collaborating with my ten-year therapist during the transition. The two even met in person. The role of the therapist in assisting with the psychotherapy made for a great combination of support. They were both concerned over the doctor switch during my demanding career. But with over thirty years in the profession, Dr. P brought enormous expertise and confidence to me, as a person with a high-profile job. She was eager to coach the coach.

As she reminded me throughout our initial interview, mood disorders cover a broad spectrum of behaviors. There are medium cases, some are severely ill, and others are beyond ill, with frequent psychosis. Triggers, and their onset role, are a real issue. There are many high-pressure occupations that can challenge the mind, just as there are regular daily pressures that can ignite imbalance in the brain. Mood disorders and the spectrum of possibilities do not discriminate between doctors, lawyers, writers, teachers, artists, police officers, coaches, entertainers, student-athletes, folks young and old. The mind has a way of operating on its own timetable regardless of a person's circumstance or profession.

"The acceptance of brain illnesses, which often elicit shame, stigma, and fear responses, depends on the level of education of people and their own life experiences," Dr. P told me. "That fear of going public and being seen in a different light scares many away from sharing their stories. This reality keeps individuals wary and sometimes seeking other methods to help with mood stabilization."

Without proper treatment, the mood disorder individual can put themselves at risk by using other methods to self-treat their condition. Often, the disease can be masked behind alcoholism and drug addiction, leading to lives of depression, violence and self-harm. Misdiagnoses and attempts to only cure the symptom, like alcoholism, and not get to the root issue leads to harm and even suicide of individuals who try and fail to escape the madness. In fact, a mood can temporarily be improved with alcohol and drugs. I was fortunate that my issues were caught due to direct episodes, and not because of a slow drip into the world of addiction. We are all vulnerable despite our biggest efforts to be bullet-proof. The life altering conditions for families and societies are clear.

"As an epidemiologist I enjoy studying patterns of distributions of disease," Dr. P said. "How much is out there and where is it? A survey study from the general population indicates that, of those incarcerated, forty to fifty percent have alcohol and/or addiction issues."

It is easy to wonder just how many of those individuals were in the undiagnosed category and found themselves acting out through life to manage their brain balance. Only more stories and education will change the landscape enough to know the answer. Prisons cannot be the gatekeepers of the undiagnosed, even when others choose a different route through self-harm and the ultimate choice of suicide. This field of medicine takes extremely insightful, intelligent people and trains them to understand the chemistry of the brain, and retrain the patient's mind. The effect of this illness, untreated, on others is inestimable.

———————

Years earlier, when I started lithium, Dr. Sally had told me that at some point it could be dangerous to my body and to my kidneys. I never really thought about it much because my health was so good, both physically and mentally. I was so absorbed in life with my family and my teams that her warning was not top of mind. But as I left Dr. Sally to go to Dr. P, tests revealed that my numbers related to my kidney function were bad.

Despite this report, I continued through the entire season to take lithium. The risk of kidney failure was certainly on my mind, but I was very committed to my team, and experienced only a few side effects. Later, after the season was over, I wondered about the greater psychological consequences if I had to switch my meds after so many years. But I decided to wait until the season ended before making a change. We had a fun and very competitive team that ripped through the first two rounds of the NCAA tournament to get to the Sweet 16. Then, the team played a very strong game against the University of Connecticut, on basically their home court as they hosted in the state of Connecticut, for a chance at another Elite Eight.

At the tournament in Athens, Georgia, I had confided to my staff about my kidney condition. There was nothing any of us could do about it, but it felt reassuring to talk openly about it. The NCAA run that year was so much fun. We had played fabulously into the Sweet Sixteen. Our thirteen-point loss to U. Conn was very disappointing, but we had battled hard against an excellent team.

Afterward, my personal fight with threatening kidney failure became my primary focus. One morning, I tried to use a sense of humor, and constructed a simple poem to explain my situation:

*My meds go up and down with not too many dramatic effects,
but my head screams about the consistent throbbing grip of
headaches. Naps abound to handle the pressure, but sleep
is not the whole measure. Lithium love has turned from a
hopeful white dove to a sinister sneaky pawn aimed at eating
my kidneys 'til dawn. No need to pout or fret, it is time to
be merry and go get the care I need to live a full life and
supersede all that is expected of me, while fulfilling all dreams
swirling from this powerful seed.*

Dr. P and I both knew it was time for me to take some time off.
When the season concluded, it was time for the medicine switch. The
plan was for me to take the month of June and retreat to northern
Michigan where I would be surrounded by friends, and could be
alone, too, and be supported by my family to handle this situation.

Still, I was concerned about others knowing my condition.
My athletic director told me he needed to inform the university
president; and he had shared the news of my bi-polar condition to his
right-hand assistant. This made me very uncomfortable. Coaches can
be authentic, but should not be seen as vulnerable, which is exactly
how I was beginning to feel, despite having been symptom-free for
almost twenty years. Absolutely nothing had occurred since my two
episodes in Maine. I had enjoyed glorious success at Michigan State,
as well as an impressive run in the postseason at Duke. So after all of
this time, I began to wonder if I was still truly bipolar. I had received
such good care that I could believe that I had been misdiagnosed, or
was just going through some phases back in Maine.

———————————

I had never revealed to any college administration about my
situation with bipolar disease. I had a huge concern over possible
discrimination, and people then scrutinizing my work unfairly
and ignorantly. Every aggressive coaching movement could be

misconstrued. Student-athletes and their parents might become concerned, or use the condition as some kind of weapon against my work. Our public figure world, and the intense coverage and sometimes unfair reporting and conjecture, is a tricky balance even with normal mental health. The strain of the season, winning and losing, and the parent and media pressures, are not for the faint of heart. I was a confident coach who felt strongly about my right to privacy as I managed my personal life well, with a great deal of support from superior doctors and a great therapist. I had added a therapist when I took on the job at Duke to ensure I had a neutral person to talk with through the ultimate challenges of the job. I also shared this information with the players when they asked about these subjects, whenever seeking personal support arose in casual conversation. I wanted them all to understand that it was okay to reach out for help. There can be so many great discussions with players that do not include basketball—on and off the court, and in and out of season.

There was one exception to keeping my medical issues private from administration. When I had my kidney issues and had to take some time off, I shared information about my condition in a conversation, regarding another matter, with an athletic department doctor. I regretted having disclosed my condition, knowing I had given up the privacy I had so cherished. Afterward, I always wondered if I was looked upon differently by the AD, his contacts, and the doctor. That loss of privacy is unrecoverable and most unsettling. I had accepted the wishes of the AD, but let my guard down with the doctor. The fear of stigma, judgmental reactions, and uninformed thoughts creep into your head as life dictates that you trust, even beyond your original sphere of privacy and comfort.

———

Going off lithium can be daunting. To help me transition from lithium to other meds, I would retreat to Michigan. I was so grateful to have special friends there. Joanie, Nate, and Melissa had been saints. We raised kids together, and shared the love of the MSU program and life in East Lansing.

My Durham tennis partners were also a great support network. They were led by Ellie, Barb, Tammy, Kathrine and Linda. Holly, my dear friend and a working woman pal, also gave me incredible love and support. My sisterly community was ready and very able to bring me through with great humor and love. From afar, five Northwestern teammates and friends, Rishal, Steph, Kris, Laura W. and Laura A., would also help with my recovery. They all knew what I faced. Now my body and brain accepted a new medical cocktail. Lithium had been simple and effective for many years, and there was no way to predict what would happen once I was off the drug. I was a blind warrior about to find out about my true self and diagnosis after twenty years.

———————————

Withdrawing from lithium started incrementally, with direct and detailed oversight by my doctor. It takes a good three weeks to get off the medication to find out where you are, before moving on with new medication, but I felt well most of the time.

There was one situation during my travels north to Michigan when I stopped by to see an old friend. She had never worked with me as my personal physician, but was aware of my condition. When I saw her that summer, she said that she thought I was trending into a hypo-manic state. I took offense at this because I didn't feel like her assertion was correct. But the more I reflected back on my behavior during the visit, I began to realize that she was right. I was a little too excitable, and my thoughts were racing. I was excited for my time in Michigan with friends, but my exuberance with her was a little over the top.

I kept in close contact with my therapist and my doctor. Both had initially expressed some concern about me going alone to Michigan. As I reflect, it was clearly not the best idea.

As my medicines changed, I had to deal with different feelings throughout each day. I had some very low times, and then some more normal times. I knew I had gotten myself into a little bit of trouble when I looked across the beautiful lake, which was so blue and clear, and told myself that I always had an escape there. I repeatedly fantasized about swimming across the Big Glen Lake in Ann Arbor as a final escape, if I ever really needed it. This may have been a low of lows, as my medication worked its way out of my system. My mind was experimenting. I was thinking deeply about my life. As disheartening as it sounds and feels to write, I was wondering about a potential escape. Recalling that singular feeling haunts me even today. Those thoughts make me think of others afflicted with bipolar disease who are struggling to put all the pieces of recovery together.

It may seem odd, but it's frequent with unbalanced mood disorders: I did not reflect too much about family, obligations, and the people I loved as I was going through such negative thoughts and my medication transition. Instead, there is a hyper focus on solving the uncomfortable feelings. After much thought, prayer, and alone time up north, and a fair amount of rain as well, which can always contribute to mood swings, I began to realize *fighting* the disease was not exactly the right strategy. Instead, I was going to have to *accept* my feelings, all of them, as a part of who I am. So many years after truly doubting my diagnosis, I had to come to grips with the idea that this disease became a part of me, and eventually I began to appreciate my mind for all of its sophistication. For the sufferer, confidence comes from knowing and believing that you are different, and even special, with your new-found gifts and creative mind. The journey is long and arduous, but the rewards and strength serve you for the rest of your life, a life well worth living, and sharing with all.

After two weeks of being sequestered in Michigan, my brain balance was in a much better place. I was age fifty-three and had made it through on my own, taking it one day at a time. To this day,

I think about why I wanted so much to be alone in those first two weeks. I felt that if I could transition alone, I could be in charge of my mind once again, while accepting that I was still bipolar, and could handle any challenge the mood disorder dared to present.

As I reflect on the entire month's experiences, I never considered myself as a person who wanted to take my life. But despair and feeling alone are a dangerous combination, as the mind swirls for direction and balance. You become trapped with your thoughts and the wonderment of your mind taking over. At times, it seems almost rational that you might choose such a direction. It seems it would bring you peace. It is heartbreaking to know that so many people, young and old, get to this breaking point without seeing a path of return to normalcy and happiness. The concept of faithful, patient endurance, with continued care and support, is the only way home.

STEPPING AWAY

After thirteen years as the head coach and women's basketball leader at Duke, I did not achieve the ultimate goal of bringing the first national championship to the program. It was a bold and lofty goal indeed, but one that I hoped for, expected—and desired emotionally. The women's program was a success and the men's team was a perennial powerhouse with, at this writing, five national championships and sixteen Final Fours under Mike Krzyzewski.

Coming from MSU and having worked with Hall of Fame coach Tom Izzo, I had been thrilled and excited to work with Krzyzewski, another Hall of Fame coach who has respectfully been called the *GOAT*—the Greatest Of All Time—in many circles. I had studied Coach K back in my Maine days and was in awe with respect, and wondered what I could learn by observing and asking questions. It seemed surreal that I could have the opportunity to go back and work alongside a mentor that I had known only from books.

During my time at Duke, Coach K was there for the big moments. I struggled early to direct the team smoothly, but the change was hard for the players. The process was filled with grief and loss for them, and building trust with a new, demanding coach was hard. Coach K banged on my door, loudly, one day to come in and said, "Do what you came here to do!"

We were about to play Rutgers, a nationally ranked team, and we were not playing well as a team, not trusting one another yet. We did win that next game, and our continuity and faith in each other began to solidify. I appreciated the push and time I spent with Coach K that day. He reached out again as we were taking on Baylor in the NCAA tourney during the Elite Eight, with a chance to go to the Final Four. The guys were in the same position. With a phone call, he reminded me that it would be very exciting for both teams to make the Final Four in the same year. In fact, I had done just that with Tom Izzo at Michigan State. We had battled one of the toughest teams, Baylor, with one of the best up-and-coming first-year players in the country. We lost by three. It was a devastating loss for us all. Ironically, at MSU during that great 2005 run, it was Baylor again that won the national title versus our Spartan team which had battled them all the way to the national title game.

Yes, there were events outside our control, such as injuries and the emotional wear and tear of some who questioned my leadership. But such things are part of the deal when you sign on to lead an elite program.

Sometimes in life, you just know that it is time for a change. I had enjoyed so much of our work at Duke. It had been an honor to serve for thirteen years. We were coming off our most exciting season ever by my standards of resilient and poised competition. Some of the early losses were painful, and playing was not up to our usual standards. But our history-making run, where we won very challenging ACC games down the stretch, and went from tenth in the league to third place, was incredible. We were led by one of the greatest players in Duke history, Haley Gorecki. We also had some great senior competitors including Haley, Kyra Lambert, Neah Odom, Emily Shubert, and the rest of the great group with Jade Williams, Jayda Adams, Mikayla Boykin, Miela Goodchild, Onome Akinbode-James, Uchenna Nwoke, Jada Claude, Jaida Patrick, Azana Baines, and Jennifer Ezeh. There was gutsy play by all. Our coaching staff and supporting staff were phenomenal as well: Jim Corrigan, Sam Miller, Wanisha Smith, Keturah Jackson, Kate Senger, Selena Castillo, Ted Kim, Ashleigh Beaver, Cat Lass and my loyal head coach assistant, Bobby Sorrell, all added special talents. It was a very inspiring staff to me. They were all warriors in the biggest sense of the word. Some media had called us the hottest team in the country due to our amazing finish, and that was fun to hear! COVID-19 would keep us from reaching our destiny because NCAA postseason play was cancelled in 2020 for all teams.

Leaving on a high note was very important to me. Our past season's success had given me such a thrill and joy, and I knew it would be a good time to pass the torch. As we all passed into the COVID bubble it became clear to me that the future seasons would be very different. All coaches would use the COVID year to develop their players further, on and off the court, with a great deal of time spent in "the bubble" together. There were so many incidents of racial injustice, and the temperature of the country had become highly polarized. I felt change was needed, not only for me, but for the university and its programs.

The reality of believing I could leave Duke came in June. John and I spoke at length about the change. I discussed it with my family and very close friends.

———————————

My family, especially Maddie and Jack, were getting comfortable with the idea that I would no longer be coaching. There had been tears of sadness and frustration. After all, your kids generally think you are the best in your field, regardless of any other circumstances. John was ready. We had given many years of our life together to this way of life, and it made sense that we were ready for new discoveries and times together. The time had come to just do it. No more talk or discussions were necessary. A calm sense of focus overcame my thinking.

There were a few things I had to do to exit in the best manner possible. Regardless of the circumstances, I believe there is way to leave a situation, a high road way to say goodbye to folks you have worked so hard with for thirteen years. My exit took a lot of thought and preparation with folks who really understood and also wanted to do things the right way.

Kate Senger and Selena Castillo were the only two staff members who needed to know in advance, and their support, loyalty, and willingness to understand, and keep things quiet so we could arrange to tell the team before any media broke the story to them, meant a great deal to me and my family.

———————

Before I decided to leave Duke, I had agreed to film a Black Lives Matter video for the team. I was looking forward to this opportunity to represent our team, and give back to them during difficult racial times. Our country was, and continues to be, hurt from pervasive racial injustices. So, anything I could do to support team members, and try to heal wounds, was especially important to me. Of course, actions speak louder than words, and filming this video was a start to a series of thoughts that began to clarify my decision to leave Duke.

The video took four hours to film. Selena and Kate were very patient as I tried to share my words carefully, with all the passion and empathy I was feeling for all persons of color. Of course, I felt inadequate in many ways as a white female who had led a sheltered and privileged life, removed from most of the racial biases and problems of equity, violence, and lack of understanding in our country. However, I did feel strongly as a leader, and I was compelled to speak on behalf of our sports program, for Duke University, and for myself.

Over the years, I had come to understand that acceptance of those who are different has a way of growing exponentially when you discover that you, too, are different. You are a smaller percentage of the whole.

As a hardworking kid from a small town, I was sheltered from many events and happenings in the real world. My friends and community were very homogenous. Independent thinking and hard work described most of the Mainers I knew and grew to love, but ethnic and sexual diversity were not a part of my early upbringing. Eventually, basketball broadened my world and opened my eyes. That round orange ball has a way that is authentic and beautiful in its ability to bring all folks together. Basketball is a very diverse sport.

I met new and different people through the sport. I would be selected to represent Maine in an international tournament in Taiwan, travelling on my own with the men's and women's teams at age sixteen. This was the first time I had met people of color, city folks, and those of different sexual orientations.

During the summer leagues in Portland, Maine, I had been asked to play on a team with older women who were gay and comfortable with it. I generally did not notice or care, but I had observed firsthand their love for the game and love for each other. They were a comical group of talented and connected woman. I looked up to them, and they enjoyed having the young kid from Brunswick on their team. Together, we won the summer league championship.

Through all my years of coaching women, one of the primary issues inside the sport was sexual orientation. The quiet fear and depression about what to do, and how to handle family and loved ones who may not understand, impacted many athletes that I coached. I could see this struggle in some who spoke with me about their pain. But there is a constant balance and private distance a coach must keep with players. To balance directive coaching with empathy is delicate. Managing emotional swings is challenging and sometimes counterintuitive to a more directive approach when framing roles or player development.

How does a coach strike the balance? Many good conversations arise, and mistakes are made, too. Learning to listen and understand a player's pain often solidified our relationship and brought it to a new level of closeness. There were many tears shared in all my offices, at all three of my schools. It was an education for me as a female coach who wanted to bring the best out of each player on and off the court. I encouraged all to be themselves, especially when dealing with parents who simply refused to understand or accept them. It is an eye-opening experience to find out that you are, in fact, an outlier to what is perceived as normal. As a person stricken with bipolar disorder, I certainly was. Any person, regardless of mental health issues, or sexual orientation, or being a racial or cultural minority, understands this place on the outside.

It was within the context of racial justice and progress that I became determined to step away from my position with the school. Duke could, with my replacement, make history by hiring a person of color. And there were certainly many strong candidates who fit the profile and had earned the opportunity. So on July 1, 2020, the first day of my final contract year, I wanted to announce my decision to leave as head coach, before the season started.

It was most important to tell the team first. I had been hoping they would be coming to campus soon so we could all talk in person. But there were delays almost each day as Duke, and all schools, as everyone tried to figure out the safest approach to bringing back the student-athletes to campus amid the novel coronavirus, which was continuing to spread. It became clear that a Zoom call was the only safe and practical method to communicate in a timely way—a disheartening reality.

Prior to my announcement, I toiled over the semantics of a press release announcing my departure. It took four edits to get the language perfect. *Retirement* was the critical word used at first. But this word just did not fit the situation. I was not choosing to *retire*, and my mind and body were far from retirement mode—a small detail to some, but a necessary clarification. This was, instead, a critical truth that needed to be shared with all, to make the story clear.

On that Wednesday morning, I first talked with the staff via Zoom and then they joined in with the team as I explained the situation. My comments were clear and from the heart. It surprised both the team and staff. I had been thinking about this very quietly, of course, and let the words just flow naturally. Very simply, I said I loved them all, and I loved coaching, but it was time for a change at Duke.

They were aware that I was heading into the final year of my contract, and there was no way I could stay on as an ineffective lame-duck coach just to collect the final year of my salary while delaying long-term growth for the program and my staff. The team's future was uncertain, and the program needed continuity and leadership.

Some of the players were emotional and others stoic, but the team and staff seemed to grasp the reasons why the change was necessary. I felt very supported. This decision was the only clear choice. There was no ill will or drama expressed. Facts were facts.

We had struggled the previous season, and I had made it clear to the team that we would not cry or become desperate about our situation. Then, we had found a way to succeed in the future—and we did. We finished the 2019-2020 season 18-12 with our very exciting run which include a 9-2 record down the stretch—good enough for third place, and the highest Duke finish to date in the new and expanded ACC.

There had been no tears as we battled back from irrelevancy to become one of the hottest teams in the country.

With my announcement at season's end, I thanked the team for the honor and privilege of serving them. I found that my emotions flooded over, and tears streamed down my face as the finality of the situation became clear. I was no longer their coach. I had in an instant, transitioned into, after thirteen years, the *former* Duke coach.

Despite the time constraints and the impending announcement to the media, my call to Coach K took place at eight on the morning of my announcement, July 1, 2020 to tell him I was stepping away from Duke. It was an emotional and raw conversation. I, as a leader, had not gotten it done. My team had stretched and driven ourselves toward winning, especially with four straight Elite Eights in the NCAA tournament, but could never get past the other enormously talented teams to reach the Final Four.

Coach K had been a major reason for me and my family choosing to come to Duke, and I wanted to tell him the news prior to the official public announcement. This morning call was much appreciated. I made it clear to Coach K that we had not achieved all of our goals, including of course, the primary goal of bringing a national title to Duke women's basketball. I was grateful to him, and the university, for my incredible opportunity. I was emotional for a moment, with the realization of the impending separation, but managed to collect myself to thank him, and his family, for all they had done for me and my family throughout the years.

Coach K was supportive, and seemed a bit caught off guard by how quickly my announcement was being made. I also was hoping to reach David Cutcliffe, Duke's head football coach, but time was winding down for us to release the video. Coach Cutcliffe had also been very good to me and my family. They felt like extended family.

We all had proudly shared in the high school graduation ceremonies of our families together. Coach K's grandchild, Coach Cut's daughter, volleyball head coach Jolene Nagel's son, and our son Jack, all graduated in the same year from Durham Academy. The great irony was that the graduation ceremonies were held on the campus of Duke's rival, UNC. We all felt a bit strange being in "enemy territory," but the photograph of all of us there together, with big smiles of pride for our families, continues to be a favorite of mine.

When a head coach steps away or is fired, there is a wake of uncertainty. Assistant coaches and staff want to know if they'll have jobs, and players wonder what role they might have under new leadership. There are no words that can ease such anxiety. Despite the uproar caused by my sudden departure, players and others expressed their support and gratitude. A letter I received from one of the players was full of joy and appreciation, and it moved me through this difficult time. It was handwritten and sent via regular mail, something you rarely see in these times of text messages, emails and social media.

It was inspiring for me to read and grasp the emotional growth and maturity of the player, an individual who, under the circumstances, showed grace and optimism. Her words will stick with me for the rest of my life. As a coach, I know that the profession is all about developing young folks, their lives, their future image of themselves as players and adults, and loving them in all ways. This includes challenging them to see their own greatness, and listening to their own cues of communication, sometimes getting them right and sometimes not. It is a two-way street, cultivated at a very fluid time for them, ages eighteen to twenty-two in most cases. It does not always work smoothly and effortlessly by both the coach and the player to get things right. It is the ultimate profession because of changing seasons, changing times, emotions fighting through reason and everyone involved trying to be their best selves, together. The words from this player put many of these thoughts together. Her letter to me will be saved forever and stay in that top drawer of reminders of what can be when people care to share and grow together. I got that letter approximately two weeks after I made my announcement.

Onome Akinbode-James has been special to me and our program since the day she arrived. She is a native Nigerian, but her family choose to have her educated in the United States. Onome is one of the bravest, most intelligent, humble, and driven people I know and have had the pleasure of recruiting and coaching. Her choice to be an engineering major at Duke exemplifies her desire to take on some of the toughest challenges offered. She is a methodical dreamer and a great thinker. We even talked with her about being president of Nigeria someday. She seeks change in her native country and I know she has the strength, leadership and conviction to make that happen.

Here are some excerpts from this treasured letter. With Onome's permission, of course, she wrote:

> *Dear Coach P,*
>
> *While we may not completely understand the politics of bureaucracy that goes into being a Head Coach, and your making of this decision, I trust that you know best and have made this tough decision after considering all things . . . I appreciate you and the impact you had on my decision to come to Duke and my time here so far . . . I remember speaking to you the first time, and knowing almost immediately that Duke was going to be my final decision. You gave me so much courage in your commitment to your players' education . . . beyond that, when I doubted my ability to compete at the ACC level, you gave me the courage to leap regardless . . . you were absolutely right . . . I cannot express into words the extent of my gratitude. You made sure I got into the right mental space while I juggled school and basketball. You have proven to be true to your words and you are such a great role model for me. You carry yourself with such power and grace and confidence . . . it was really hard watching your breakdown today. Sometimes in the crazy world of a basketball season, we tend to get caught up in our emotions of the coaching and forget about the human behind the role. I have talked to my host family and shared with them that I never would have come to Duke without you.*
>
> *Thank you for supporting me and all my causes, thank you*

for allowing me to play basketball on the ACC stage, thank you for being a steadfast believer, thank you for standing your ground and staying true to yourself even when you received criticism . . . thank you for teaching me to speak up more, both for myself and for my community, thank you for getting me to stop apologizing for nothing, thank you for treating me as your daughter . . . you will always hold a special place in my heart. I promise to keep working and pushing hard for you. My mom sends her regards and always regards to your family
    —Love, Onome

These words helped me transition away from coaching at the time of my departure better than anything ever could. I have never received a letter as long or involved as Onome's. She and one of her teammates, Jen Ezeh, raised over $5,000 for their nonprofit, Covid Fund Naija, for their home country. We all have donated to the cause and support both Onome and Jen in every way. There are simply no limits for a person with Onome's character and heart. She is a warrior in all ways as she is a fighter for great ideas and causes, and she seeks that incredible healthy balance in life to achieve at the highest level. I will follow her career on and off the court with great anticipation and love for her, and her dreams.

PART TWO

STACEY

Sometimes things happen in ways that can change your life forever. Stacey Porrini, one of my former players at the University of Maine and an exceptional individual and leader, had breast cancer for many years. We all thought she could win her most difficult battle. Then we all learned that the cancer returned. After an incredible warrior-like mentality towards her disease, Stacey P, as we affectionately called her, passed away. She was a mother of two, a dear wife, a dear sister, aunt, and daughter. I can remember being at the funeral with my former players from the University of Maine. I was struck by how this terrible thing could happen to somebody so young, and seemingly healthy in every way. Stacey left behind a wonderful husband, two beautiful children, a dear family and friends who admired her greatly. Stacey was a gifted, giving and faithful person.

Stacey had been my first home visit when I became head coach at Maine. This is a special time in the recruiting process where the coaches from all interested schools can visit the homes of prospective student-athletes. I can still remember the wonderful Italian meal her mom cooked to welcome us into her home. I remember watching her at swim practice. Her fluid strokes were so impressive and powerful. I was amazed how her six-foot four-inch frame could cruise through the water so effortlessly. She was the epitome of health throughout her career. She exuded a healthy mind and body in every way. She fought so hard with her cancer battle, while trying to uplift others as well.

After her cancer's return, she was gone in a matter of weeks. Stacey had continued to teach her young students right up until she departed earth. I can see her family walking down the aisle after the service, especially her youngest, her daughter Olivia. Olivia was crying as she reached for the hand of her grandmother. She was going to grow up without her mom which made me pause, cry deep tears, and feel profoundly sad. Sitting together, and crying with my former Maine players, was healing, and also very compelling. That day reminded me so much of what we can do in this life in terms of sharing, mentoring, and growing through our own experiences. None of us could ever have imagined that we would be sharing such a life-altering moment. One of us, one who had battled beside us and for her family, was gone.

There is a natural order of things that, when interrupted, can be shocking and surreal. Personally, I felt a strong sense of reality hit me in the face: aI had struggled with my own issues of life appreciation, and here Stacey had fought for hers, until her last breath. One cannot minimize one's own experiences, but the sanctity of life and its gift is one of the clear thoughts that keeps circling through my mind.

Stacey's passing changed me forever. I sat with others in the church, and we were reminded that life is imperfect and unpredictable. I never dreamed I would be at one of my players' funeral. We all struggled with this reality that no one could believe or control. While in the church I began to think of my life differently. My life experiences had been hidden within me for too long. I wondered what Stacey would have thought of me had she known my whole story. What would she say? I can almost hear her say, *"Coach, we appreciate you just as you are."* Or, *"Coach P, we do not care about your situation, we love you and appreciate you as a coach."*

Stacey had used similar words with me during other circumstances as I coached her throughout her career. She was a rare student-athlete who appreciated lessons and coaching. Most of us need to step away for a while before we really understand the lessons taught by our mentors, but Stacey absorbed learning on the spot, motivating me to share my story. I wondered whether my motivational reach went beyond the basketball court. Stacey was no longer on this earth to teach her students or create her own story with her family. But I was blessed to be here still.

That entire day of the funeral I felt a pull to do something and do more. *Life is too short,* I thought. *How could I make Stacey proud? How could I be as strong a warrior as she had been?*

———————

Later that summer, a dear friend of mine, a former teammate and her family, lost their daughter, Courtney. Courtney took her own life. She was a tender and beautiful young person. Her passing challenged me think even further about my place on this earth. So much tragedy in a short period of time, affecting the lives of people I loved and who made a difference to me. The facts about each situation were not comparable, but the message was familiar, loud and clear. It was all about joy in honoring these wonderful women, and understanding their separate stories, and then learning from the raw emotions remaining after their loss.

To see my teammate Connie and her family in that church that day made me want to run outside and scream. There was just so much pain for everyone, and the sadness was unbearable despite the family's smiles of gratitude for all the support. I felt guilty, but for what? I wasn't sure until days, weeks and months had passed. *Perhaps,* I would conclude, *I could have done more.*

So many young people take their own lives. Healthy, beautiful, young people are finding their own methods of escape. The loneliness shared by any person who chooses such a path is unendurable. I could not help wondering what Courtney was feeling and thinking when she decided to depart life here on earth.

Courtney's mom and my teammate, Connie, had been a source of great strength for me when I was just a young freshman at

Northwestern University, finding my way through big-time college athletics. Connie's husband and two sons are remarkable people with an incredible faith. Watching that great family dynamic created a disconnect for me: how and why could Courtney be gone so young and in this way? More questions and few answers for all, and for me personally.

As the hymns played and the prayers were spoken, I could not stop thinking about what could be done in the future to honor Courtney and her family. I had so much experience to share. How could I find an outlet to bring attention to others about the issues of the mind? Could the stigmas and the current state of acceptance of mental health issues stand in my way?

Stacey and Courtney's funerals, in their own way, pushed something deep inside me much closer to the surface. The loss of two lives, far too young. Two funerals within three months. Spiritual and practical thinking, while celebrating the lives of both women, occupied my thoughts continuously. Stacey and Courtney had never met, yet their independent stories rattled me from the inside out, while calling me to consider more about what I was offering to the world as I knew it.

———————

My dear friend James Mitchell had accompanied me on the trip to Courtney's funeral. Mitch had served as a mentor to Duke football while coaching both of Courtney's brothers at Duke. Mitch provided great support to both programs at Duke, and he always got me thinking. I wanted a way to promote mental health, and help reduce the stigma around all mental health diseases.

The first thought that came to my mind was to have an annual *Mental Wealth* game at Duke. We had wonderful fans who enjoyed the grassroots approach of using a great sport like women's basketball for noble causes. Oddly to me, however, I received some pushback for the idea of using the team to bolster mental health in this manner.

As I approached some potential sponsors for the game, I was not met with full support. I found this striking, but revealing. I also spent time talking to fellow coaches. Very few, if any, wanted to take on mental health or promote mental well-being around their programs at that time. Such hesitancy can be natural at first. The *how* and *why*, and ability to relate the parts of mental health to our day-to-day living, is a challenge. The stigmas are real, and many people are not comfortable entering the mental health arena. Still, women's basketball is a great venue to educate and expose folks to the pieces that serve mental health so that more of the whole can be understood.

We forged ahead with terrific support from the athletic department, community, and team. Many of us have experienced coping with someone else's mental health issues. There have been young people trying to escape their mental challenges who choose to deal with them by themselves. It can be in college or high school, or anywhere.

After reaching out to the ACC, I was able to observe and participate in the ACC mental wellness weekend in Raleigh. It was heartbreaking to listen to the parents of a young person who decided to take his life. Once again, I was emboldened to try to do something to make a difference while I was coaching, and perhaps after my coaching career as well.

The second year of the event, we were able to secure some beautiful shoes donated by Kyrie Irving, the famous NBA star. The team wore them proudly during the game. The shoes were sharp, with both Duke blue and green. The official color for mental health is green, and it blended well with our Blue Devil blue. The team was so happy to receive these great shoes from such a special person who played at Duke, and had displayed such integrity throughout his career. On the concourse, we had all sorts of mental wealth events to promote wellness.

We had speakers come both years. Chamique Holdsclaw, a former WNBA player who also played for, and won, national championships with Pat Summit at Tennessee, was our first guest speaker at the inaugural game. Chamique is truly special as she was able to share her life with schizophrenia, which had been diagnosed while she was an incredibly successful collegiate basketball player. Cherokee Parks, a former Duke men's basketball player, spoke the second year sharing stories, educating, and answering questions from fans prior to the game. Both speakers were so authentic and helpful. Their willingness to share and speak their own truth with grace and confidence made each Mental Wealth game uniquely special.

Each year I was even more grateful for the time that we could spend raising awareness. I was so pleased to have Courtney's parents, Connie and Kelby, as guests to the game in honor of their beautiful daughter.

It seems like such a small thing, but when people realize you can talk openly and comfortably about such a difficult subject, even with all stigmas and stories attached, you have reached a special place in the hearts of many. I could feel a connection to all involved. The honesty and integrity of the stories made my heart full, and motivated me more than ever. Exposing the team to such great athletes, leaders and their shared stories made each experience truly special, while providing a subtle opportunity for anyone potentially affected to feel safe and surrounded by care.

It is fair to say that most of my adult life has been consumed with coaching. There is a season to every year of coaching, and the beauty of not knowing what each season will bring.

The older I get, the more writing and thinking I do about how we can impact lives more broadly through women's basketball. We have an opportunity through our sport to make a difference in ways far beyond merely winning games or hoisting trophies.

Women's basketball is a great venue to reach out and support all causes. There are so many organizations that benefit from their alignment with the sport. At all the schools where I have coached, we have organized and connected with groups that can benefit women's health and health for all. We also have done some work with melanoma. One of my players at Duke had, at twelve, lost her mother to melanoma. We became heavily invested in the Polka Dot Mama Foundation as part of the Melanoma Research Alliance. I am proud to be a board member, and to share my own personal stories about melanoma, and how it often takes so many young lives. We, as a program, were doing things to bring the community together, and to make a difference.

INNER CIRCLE

The impact on family life of being the head coach of a major basketball program can be extraordinary. I was extremely fortunate in that John was very supportive and able to handle the grueling pace of my schedule, along with the unending physical and emotional demands on our marriage and children. My family was blessed to have a tight inner circle of friends and family who helped to backstop us and provide uncompromising support.

John had to navigate a world he had never dreamed would be such a major part of our lives. He has had to endure the sleepless nights, observe his wife in altered states of mental health in my early career, and study feverishly about bipolar disorder and its lifetime effects on me and our family. For long periods, John needed to monitor me and stay closely by my side. He had to take on the professional worries as well. He knew I loved coaching, but with the wrong information and lack of support, my career could have been in jeopardy. He was protective and very private, and always leery of the public figure aspect of my work. These concerns were magnified greatly as we raised Maddie and made plans to have our second child, Jack.

John was deeply committed to raising our children and balancing his teachings and academic study of economics, while staying strong for me. His logical scientific mind and chemistry background was a godsend because he understood how chemicals can change in the brain. He sought private advice from a few dear trusted friends. I am amazed to this day the emotional and mental strength he exhibited throughout the challenges. He is the quiet hero of our family. He kept his steady resolve through the darkest times. John's tight grip, quiet words of reassurance, and soothing reason were a large part of our dark nights together. Some of those nights seemed endless. The stamina he showed for coping with my suffering was beyond impressive.

The children were carefully protected. John did express his wonder of genetics, and whether the children would have to cope in a similar fashion. Only time, and continued observation and thoughtful preparation, can help ease our anxiety about their future mental health.

To this day, we still harbor concerns that our children, now adults, may one day exhibit bipolar symptoms. When Maddie tells us she had a sleepless night, my own anxiety rises. When Jack shared with us that he too was struggling with sleep while in college, I became deeply anxious and concerned because sleep deprivation had been a trigger point for my battle with mental illness. I try not to project my behaviors or anxieties onto my daughter and son, but lingering within me is the concern that I may have genetically influenced their mental health. We are, as a family, educated and aware. Faith takes over from here.

———

Friends can come into your life for many reasons and it is a true joy when the friendships last a lifetime. Helping John through the initial tough times in Maine were Terry and Stan. We met them during our second year at the university in Orono. We were close from the start, even prior to having kids. We played golf together, and they were avid supporters of the team. Terry is the kind of friend who sat with Maddie in the waiting room as I gave birth to Jack, answering Maddie's continual questions of "Why?" and "When?" with loving patience. Stan and John spend many hours on the golf course honing their skills with side bets and cigars. The couple friendship has lasted over twenty-five years and is still going.

Terry and Stan were there the day we played golf during that challenging fall surrounding my first episode. They all knew I was off mentally. Fortunately, both Terry and Stan had worked in social work and counseling. They continued to play without approaching me or questioning my motives. But, through their life experiences they knew more. They helped John through that day, and our friendship took a much deeper turn from that point forward. In them, John had two confidants. Terry and Stan understood. Together they worked to solve the issue while sharing many private conversations. Sadly and ironically, years later, Terry confided in me that she had witnessed this dreaded disease firsthand in a close family member. He had taken his life years ago. I was stunned.

Terry had lived a life of knowing, because a dear and talented person close to her wanted to escape the pain and did so violently. I was very fortunate to have such enlightened friends in my corner. They were educated in many mental health issues. Terry also helped me take my meds and craft a life filled with support from other women. Terry had introduced me to Mary Margaret, my acupuncturist friend. I will never underestimate the value of a tight-knit circle of support where women take the lead role.

———————————

Maddie, our bright-eyed and enthusiastic daughter with a huge sense of life, carried on with her Montessori school in Orono, and riding horses at the barn down the road. She and I spent many hours with our beloved "Fancy Face." Maddie's childhood was filled with many different experiences. She had moved from Maine to Michigan and then to North Carolina before turning thirteen. She struggled with the move to Duke. She had great longtime friends in Michigan and had really enjoyed her soccer and basketball teammates there.

I kept her close during the move and even had her travel with me to Europe to coach during that time. She loved the team and our closeness with the wonderful people of USA Basketball. They all were a welcome distraction from moving house, and great support. Defeating Russia on their home court for the gold medal and sharing that experience with Maddie was memorable for me, too.

Maddie began to adjust to her new life in Durham. She picked her own high school, after a year at Durham Academy as an eighth grader. She loved her three years at the public school down the road, Riverside High School. She finished her collegiate career at Elon College, playing ball with some great teams, and then returned to get her MBA.

I had waited many years to talk with Maddie about my condition. When she was twenty-one I felt it was time for her to know the extent of my illness. Maddie did not know about my condition and taking lithium, or my status as a bipolar coach.

I kept it brief, but tried to educate her as fully as possible. Naturally, she wondered if it could be a part of her DNA. We had never seen any signs, but many times the disease reveals itself in the later twenties or early thirties. Maddie was proud of me and glad to know more fully what I had been dealing with for more than two decades. I felt relieved in her knowing.

A few years later we got into a discussion in more detail about my time in the hospital. I became emotional, even after all those years. Many tears flowed, and it was Maddie who took the parent role. As I slid down the wall, weak-kneed and sobbing, I shared some of the more difficult details of my hospital stay during my first episode. I was so grateful for Maddie's support and empathy, and I am so proud of the confidence and poise she exudes every day.

Ironically, Jack, our lithium child, is the brightest of our bunch. He has shown no signs of being hindered by the chemicals flowing through me while he was *in utero*. He dedicated himself to his studies throughout high school and enrolled in my alma mater, Northwestern University.

The neuroscience and other details regarding his different entry into this world will always mystify us. I would like to have been a part of a research study while pregnant with Jack. Of course, it appears that it would still be scientifically impossible or improbable to ascertain the inside workings of the fetus' mind. Jack continues to be our medical miracle, busy with a very exciting life.

Interestingly enough, and perhaps predictably, I ended up being a bit of a hovering mom with Jack. I worried about his growth and development. I wondered if there were any side effects for a child where the mom has taken lithium throughout the pregnancy. I was certainly accused by Maddie, on more than one occasion, that I babied him. This is fair and true. Because I had miscarried after Maddie, I wondered if having another baby was truly prudent and possible. Once Jack arrived, it took me more time to let go of the worry. He chose to go away from Durham for college, a good decision that reflects his independence and confidence.

———————————

My family, along with many other special individuals who have been a part of my mental health experiences, created quite a team. These committed individuals, through their choice or not, are incredibly inquisitive and have been committed to a championship mentality when it comes to the shared adversity of the situation. This is an ultimate team of courage-laden folks who put others before themselves: they have strived to understand the whys of mental health, and the assault that mental illness can have on someone they care for and love. Successfully managing the disease and having a productive, happy life makes the good moments even better. And, thanks to my medical team and family, we have had lots to smile about.

Having proof of brain balance from meds, despite the normal anxieties of life, is key to acceptance of mood disorders. In one week at Michigan State, I was asked to carry the winter Olympic torch, move into a beautiful office complex for the team and staff, and play a top-ten team at home, televised on CBS Sports. Such excitement can trigger the manic mind, even when the meds are working. But despite poor sleep that week, I was able to cope and even thrive. We defeated that undefeated top-ten team soundly the day after my no-sleep evening. It illustrated that my disorder is just a part of me. That one evening, and lack of sleep, proved to be one of the most fortifying experiences for me with my brain health. I was more than okay, and I coached one of the best games of my career. I was sharper than ever, and able to celebrate the torch run and the dominant victory. It had been our first nationally televised game for the program since my arrival. I was normal. Sleepless nights were nothing for me to fear anymore.

HEART SPACES

The following chapter contains excerpts from interviews with some of my extended family members. The very thoughts, from members of my family whose daughter was diagnosed with bipolar approximately five years ago, share the pain and the triumph I know so well. There had been continued speculation within our family about the origin of my bipolar gene, and whether it would surface again, and then this young woman was diagnosed. Such a life-altering challenge is personal to all involved. There is no way to dampen the worry and concern that follows. She was in high school, so much younger than I was at the time of my diagnosis.

I marveled at her strength and was crushed by her darkness. I wanted to help her in any way possible. Initially it was very hard to help her. She was caught in the medicine discovery world. It's most frightening when a child loses hope and perspective. Many will choose to escape their world. The following passages describe a real-life experience with a bipolar teenager and how the story plays out for many families.

———————

A mother finds her middle child on the bedroom floor with pill bottles spilled and the contents consumed. The child is barely awake and her mind has been altered considerably. Immediate phone calls start the trail of confused and incoherent communication. Mom can hardly speak to her husband on the phone. There are no words to explain what is occurring. A neighbor bounds over to the house, barefoot in the snow. Husband races home, not understanding what exactly he is facing, but fearing the worst. The ambulance arrives and there is panic and the unknowing. Parents are frozen. Daughter is whisked away, while Mom stands frozen in time. The arrival at the psychiatric ER room is surreal. The room is meticulously white with absolutely nothing in it to pose a threat. IV cords, mirrors, flower vases, are removed.

A stranger serves as a guard outside the room. There is very little communication at this point. Feelings start to pour out of the parents. Total sadness, shock, anger, and embarrassment flood their minds. *How could she do this? Why does she not appreciate our life together?* Immediate guilt and blame set in. Shame about what is happening, while not knowing what is happening, collides with blame to form an unbelievable physical and emotional pain. Stomachs churn and the mom cannot stop crying. *Who can we call?* Mom calls her sister, giving no real clarity and sobbing directly into the phone. Mom cannot and will not alert her own mother who lives in the area. There is too much pain and no emotional resolution, so she cannot be bombarded with questions no one can answer.

The transfer to another mental health facility begins. Dad rides in the ambulance with his daughter. A man of great faith, he is overwhelmed by this reality. He turns silent. Unable to respond to his daughter, he is also unsure how to comfort her as well. Mom withdraws and shuts out her friends. As a stay-at-home mom, failure comes to her mind. Awkwardness and shame wrap around every thought. *As a mom how could I reach out? What would I say? What would they think?* Oddly, as the daughter is admitted, a high school friend of Mom's says hello. The old friend works at the facility. The moment is ironic, surreal, and a part of life in a small town, yet with the mom's incredibly swollen and tear-stained face, and with her clearly pained dark eyes, she stares blankly at this stranger. The family is not alone. A boy in the hall cries out repeatedly, "I wanna go home." His words are haunting and unforgettable. Another patient, a girl, was admitted because her father pushed her down a flight of stairs. She is pregnant.

Mom and Dad think this must be a dream. Just a day ago all seemed right in the world for the whole family. *How were we in this place?* Blessings can find their way to the most estranged situation and places. Casey, the caseworker in charge, introduced herself. She emanated a confidence and care that was desperately needed. She exuded warmth and hope within the chaos. *How can our daughter be so brave and stay overnight here?*

There was a shortage of beds. The daughter's roommate was a recently admitted eight-year-old. Therapy sessions would begin on Friday, but the Thanksgiving holiday weekend prevented weekend sessions and therapy. Mom takes a strong stance and demands to take her daughter home. There were evaluations and papers signed, and then the family returns home, together, against the judgment of those at the hospital. Mother's intuition and need for control arrives in full force. The house has to be secure. An entire cleanup takes place. No knives, no razors, scissors, cords, and all medication collected. A safe is purchased just to keep things out of sight.

Outpatient care begins after the holiday weekend. Mom is determined to be there. Time passes and plans are made for recovery. Mom sleeps with her daughter every night for a year. Complications with sleep and emotional reactions abound. Cutting comes into the equation as the brave daughter clamors for a sense of control. Mom becomes a shadow lurking around every corner. Parents are horrified their daughter would cut on herself. Self-inflicted painful cuts and bloodied arms become part of the story. Family therapy begins in full force as they circle the middle child who needs all the family's energy and attention.

Two other daughters feel lost and beyond sad. There are no immediate answers. It seemed best to hide the detailed information from the youngest daughter. The oldest immediately takes on the burden and blame, but she does not know why. There is not time to know exactly the correct path in handling the family. Due to the nature of the middle daughter's mania and her actions, the father cannot cope. "We failed her," he says aloud.

Healing begins, but there are many challenges as the entire family struggles with knowing how to balance accountability for her, and being terrified of the next incident. Hearing her talk is very important. But hearing her descriptions of frightening impulse behavior is excruciating.

"What would it be like if I ran a red light and drove into a wall?"

The irrational nature of her thoughts is overwhelming each day. With the car promptly taken away, and adjustments being managed daily, more questions appear. *When do you tell someone you are bipolar?* the mind immediately asks and wants to know. *How will it impact the people around me? What will they really think? When will I ever feel comfortable taking these medications?* These and other daunting thoughts arise in a high school girl just wanting to be normal again.

Parents sort through the wonderment of all things new. *How do we get the doctors and therapists to work together?* There are competing thoughts that confuse all. Mom and Dad question the doctors and wonder about the label assigned to her diagnosis. Mom is a tough sell and wants to really know what applies to her middle daughter. It takes time for both parents to accept, after observing more behaviors, that the bipolar label appears accurate.

Aftershocks are very real. Other schoolkids taunt her with personal jeers about her past while she is playing basketball. There are calls from the parents to the high school athletic directors to seek help in giving their daughter respect. Other family members comment subtly that her parents were too hard on her. The blame game is a constant theme. There is faith in God, but too many questions. Balancing faith and prayer with the devices of science and understanding seems impossible, and they sometimes collide.

The affluent town is filled with parents jockeying with their kids to get into the best colleges. There is that wonderful anxiety of hyper-focused parents: concern over applications, résumés, and only the absolute best for each child. Conversations become hard to handle, given the simple nature of those issues. Tolerance is low with many in public settings or at games or other school functions. Life goes on but it is never the same. Somewhere down the road, with great care and medical planning, things begin to change.

The young, creative student-athlete earns a scholarship to play basketball at a Division I university. She suffers knee injuries and more challenges with a different kind of rehabilitation and recovery. She battles through each experience. She graduates a semester early. Her photography business is booming due to her truly authentic photographs. She has many friends and an empathetic way that is beyond her years. A special trip to Africa with her mom nourishes her soul. There, witnessing the joy of so many who have so little in their lives, brings a perspective to her world. She knows how fortunate she is to see the world through a different prism of life. Her meds and her experiences are working in concert to show her this new and remarkably successful world. She is better than ever. She rises from her seat in a lecture hall at a major university, in front of all the student-athletes, when the question is posed to the group about anyone suffering from impaired mental health. The question is asked and there is silence. No one raises their hand or speaks. Then, there is the daughter, this young woman, showing more bravery than her parents could imagine at the time, as she stands and volunteers, "I do."

Experimenting with her doctors to find the right balance takes time and belief in the diagnosis. Her questions are real and personal. She had always had a sound mind and did well physically with sports. She struggled early under the most difficult circumstances. The thought of those desperate actions coming to fruition for her family is crushing and unfathomable. Her parents work the delicate balance of her treatment and privacy while observing her 24/7.

———————

I admire the parents so much. Observing is a delicate task.

Too many questions becomes isolating and intimidating. Quiet support and love are tricky to balance in the world of suicide. It is your child. When a child is sick with the flu or otherwise, of course you know what to do. No one can be prepared for the mind of a child suffering. But we all need to hear the stories, learn the signs, educate each other and celebrate the incredible success stories of pain and triumph. There are so many incredibly inspiring stories to tell.

Poor mental health is serious and filled with unknowns. Shame deepens quickly. Parents feel responsible but cannot fathom how they are here, and what exactly is happening. Shame is a daily feeling for the suffering, and escaping the stigma of shame is crucial to moving forward.

When I was able, I repeatedly said to her that, "It is not your fault." Wise words from times past, and now mine to share. This daughter has many talents. Our conversations focus on how special her brain is, and the capacity she has for brilliant things.

As a photographer, she can see the angles of beauty in almost anything. She has a brilliance and creativity about her that is beyond special. In this way, we talk about us both having the gift. We are gifted in ways that many cannot understand. Our closeness and understanding grows richer and deeper each day. We talk meds sometimes. We can joke about the bad side effects and the changes we are making to have a better fit for our meds and minds. We share a special place. We do not overthink the originations of our genetic pools anymore. We stand alone in our own way. Together, we are free.

MOVING TARGETS

Families with a history of disease worry about future generations. No one wishes to pass any illness on to their children or their children's children. The mental health gene brings that same fear of acceptance to the table. *Who is next? Will it skip a generation? What about grandchildren? Is there anything I can do to avoid the* Beautiful Mind *life sentence?*

The diagnosed and their families initially do not want to face the possible realities. The lack of control they feel—their helplessness—can be traumatizing.

Verbiage becomes critical in communication from doctor to patient. The affected prefer to hear the words "mood disorder," as the other, more typical labels are generally received in a pejorative manner. Many of us can accept poor mental health in others, but when it strikes too close to home, the feelings of acceptance are much more challenged. Sometimes the more uneducated or less sensitive will refer to the afflicted as "crazy," or that "they have lost their minds."

Despite such social stigmas, healthy productive living with a mental disease is possible and far more common than one might think. The truth is, nearly one in five adults lives with mental illness. In the US, that's nearly fifty million people.

A balanced brain and life are possible through a diversified portfolio of solutions. The search for joy often can come through simple action, like pet ownership and consistent sleep cycles. Organized and simple lives are important. Cognitive restructuring of the mind to accept and grow with the new normal can be effective. Every part of the coaching and cognitive re-tooling of the message can be a valuable part of the medical care.

"The work of the world does not wait to be done by perfect people," a doctor once told me. This statement provides comfort, strength, and motivation to move forward.

As one learns more about a diagnosis, there are countless reminders of the brilliant and famous people who have been diagnosed and yet led incredible lives, in most cases. Ernest Hemingway, Frank Sinatra, Winston Churchill, Vivian Leigh, Carrie Fisher. Many have surmised that Vincent van Gogh also suffered through the madness of mood swings. This is special company, and serves as a reminder of the power of the brain and how we can reshape the thinking of those who suffer, and how they can succeed brilliantly as well.

There are many sad stories about outcomes of people with mood disorders. But there are more successes, I am certain. We don't hear as much about those. My accomplishments hinged on getting great medical care and a network of support, which led to my own acceptance and peace with my journey. I was able to see directly how improved I was as a human being.

My success stories, and those of others, are not perfect by any measure, but they give hope and peace to those suffering. Among the positive messages to be shared are that there have been steady breakthroughs in prescription medicines. The benefits-to-side effects ratio is getting better.

One of the treatments that saved me early on was the lithium. I have been fascinated by the its development back in the 1970s. Lithium was clearly a missing element in my brain balance. Taking a lithium supplement stabilized me, made me highly functional in my job, and allowed me to be a loving normal parent to my children, and wife to my husband.

As discussed earlier, I was placed on lithium initially because another medicine I was taking was potentially harmful to me and could have caused birth defects in any future children. I was experiencing headaches, weight gain, and memory lapses. It took a wonderful doctor to get me on the right track physically and emotionally.

Dr. Sally helped me learn more and feel confident with my switch to lithium. Such long-term learning makes you feel as if you have studied a bit in medical school. When I had to stop taking the drug, we came up with another regimen that worked. Having a doctor who understands you and stays by your side is crucial to managing mental illness. I could not have asked for a better medical partner than Dr. Sally.

It is hard to put into words her intellect, skill, and ability to sort through all problems of the mind and its balance. Accessibility and finding a doctor you truly click with is so important. As she said many times, "The mind is where you are living." She has been working on issues of the mind for over thirty years, and her success rate with finding solutions to a myriad of mental health issues is astounding. She is hard-wired for empathetic listening.

Dr. Sally once shared a story from her medical school days about the man suffering from PTSD. He initially said (in the example) that he was "ready to pull the trigger." After much evaluation and assessment, she learned how to manage such threats and simply gave the dry, confident response to the example, "I will see you tomorrow." Dr. Sally, even in her learning years, proposed a simple strategy to that example patient by planning three- and four-times-a-week visits, each time getting him to commit to the next visit, thus restructuring his mindset and thinking right on the spot.

Sometimes it is word choices made by the doctor that are so critical. The action a doctor takes can also promote confidence over worry. Both matter greatly.

Mental health impairment can be so frightening, and cause one to recoil. The experienced doctors can defuse even the most serious threats and comments. Alarmism can be prevalent, and rightly so, because of the family's worries and concerns.

During my therapy, the consistency of a doctor's actions, and time, was a huge piece in finding the root of my brain imbalance. Dr. Sally would challenge me to follow simple tasks, and would ask questions that required my personal commitment to my therapy. She reviewed the meds with me by asking pointed questions about my dosages, and when I was taking them. She repeatedly asked me if had picked up my meds at the drugstore. Actually, John picked up my medicine for years because I continued to fight for privacy, and had to remain wary that because of my public figure status I would be recognized picking up those meds. It seems funny now. Of course, my name was clearly labeled on the bottles.

Dr. Sally would evaluate my hands, especially my fingernails. At times, when I was initially struggling, my nails were bitten down so far that they would bleed. They did not exactly represent a calm, non-anxious focus. When I truly acquiesced and followed patterns and certain behavior requests by my doctor, I was well on my way to developing trust, and then, finding the truth. With Dr. Sally securing commitment upon commitment from her patient, my road to success became clearer. Time, observation, discussion, and medical treatment are the healers.

Dr. Sally's humor always helped me perceive things differently. The dialect of empathic thinking, combined with the full knowledge of the brain chemicals, is an incredible gift and well-seasoned craft. She remarked that she uses a spreadsheet from the very beginning with each patient. Others' opinions, whether it be family or other doctors, are noted, but she starts fresh with each patient. She trusts her patients and gets a thrill when they become independent, good learners relative to their own brain balance.

Dr. Sally tells a story of a conversation with a chief resident during her medical school days. They were discussing her future and all the choices in front of her regarding the medical field:

"Sally, you are smart enough to do anything. It seems psychiatry is the ultimate fit and most challenging field. It suits you."

This statement speaks to the value of those doctors who can see inside the brain with empathetic dialect, the incredible science of statistical fluctuations in treatment, brain chemical expertise, and emotional elements that run deep within where we live: our minds.

As I became accustomed to life with lithium, and was reticent to change medications despite my kidney issues, Dr. Sally and her therapeutic words rang clear once again. I was so sold on the fact that lithium is a natural salt found on the periodic table of elements. Somehow, this scientist thinking gave me comfort in my medicine being "real" and safer than others, and perhaps a special element for some bodies and brains. With her empathetic tone and sardonic delivery, Sally said, "Don't kid yourself. Natural does not mean safe. Have you ever heard of arsenic?"

Lessons I learned from Dr. Sally are numerous. She taught me how to think differently about my disorder by understanding the science of the mind. The inexact nature of it all was made clear. I did not have to be perfect, but my quality of life could be better than ever. She showed me that I could be a mom with a lifelong mood disorder. She was a rock as I took my lithium daily while pregnant, expressing fears about my son's health on each visit. She saw many, many tears.

My respect for my doctors and their mind-altering therapies could not be any greater. Their insights and understanding of the brain, and how it works, coupled with their ability to communicate so clearly with the patients, is an incredible combination. A psychiatrist friend once shared with me that the overall respect and financial compensation are lower for practitioners in the psychiatric field. Their work is not viewed always as life-saving and urgent by some. My experiences have taught me that this field of medicine is really the widest specialty as it encompasses all aspects of health—physical and mental. The work should be esteemed and valued as lifesaving and urgent in every way. A free mind is the best antidote to all illnesses.

The transition of docs for me was rather impressive. Dr. Sally slowed down but held the baton just long enough to execute a seamless handoff to Dr. P.

As emphasized by Dr. P, this care team made no assumptions as they developed a clear picture together. Dr. P became my next medical partner, helping me, as Dr. Sally had, to understand my condition and the science behind my treatment regimen. Good doctors observe a patient's physical presentation closely. *Are the palms sweaty? Does the patient appear relaxed or tense? Are they looking at their feet or making eye contact?* Listening skills might be the most important attribute to any patient/doctor relationship. The doctor listens to the cadence of the speech and notes whether the patient presents a cogent and coherent speech pattern. Observation is a critical part of the analysis of behavior, and the methods and meds that lead to recovery.

The delicacy in finding the right medical cocktail is fascinating. The brain is so sensitive. Small changes in meds make a big difference in mood outcomes. All brains are uniquely different, which is why patients must be viewed as such and observed so closely. For example, a change in my sleep and mood can be improved by tweaking the dosage of a prescription. I have long been amazed at how physicians make such determinations. It's made me appreciate the folly—and danger—of self-medicating. I have been guilty of this dangerous behavior a few times. Thankfully, I was reeled back in by both my doctors.

It's vital to understand that mood disorder and thought disorder are different illnesses requiring different treatments. The mixing of diagnoses can create a situation where a patient moves between the two. Bipolar I and II can also be one in the same, at times. Labels are tricky. I fluctuated at times as being both. Dr. P educated me to recognize the difference. Bipolar I and II differ in the severity of manic episodes. The mood-thought disorder is even trickier. Thought disorders can involve a complete dissociation with reality to the point of hallucinations and a lost sense of reality. There is quite a spectrum and continuum to identify for each patient. Mania distorts the patient's brain so there is simply not an accurate accounting of the world.

I have settled in with the use of Lamotrigine, Clonazepam and Trazadone. Lamotrigine is an anti-seizure medicine. Trazadone is a non-addictive sleep aid, and Clonazepam is another anti-seizure medicine to help calm electrical activity in the brain. It does not interact poorly with other medications. It stimulates the GABA receptors—gamma amino butric acid. Interesting medical terms, indeed. For me it is simple: together, these three combine to give me exactly the med support I need to handle all types of stressful situations. Given the potential complications, it is a miracle to me that my doctors can so precisely fine-tune my medical regimen. I dare not think of a life without them.

WISE WORDS

As an elite women's basketball coach, many mornings I would text my team, or send individual messages to help direct them. I wrote much about fear and failure and rising to the occasion many times. These texts were more prevalent during our times of difficulty. All of my words were intended to motivate and restructure thinking as we persevered. The following are messages I sent to my Duke student-athletes:

TO THE TEAM:
"Good Morning. Here's to a great Monday. It is fun to work on developing a "full life." Of course, that means different things to different people. But it always means rising above circumstances beyond your control. Keep trying to move past any painful memories or experiences: that's always a key to staying in the present and moving forward."

TO ONE SPECIAL PLAYER WHO BATTLED ADVERSITY HER ENTIRE CAREER:
"Reminder to face adversity with confidence and firm determination. Expect to encounter hardships as you journey towards all of your dreams and interests. Sometimes it is a very broken world. This is why bravery is needed. Bravery and hope in all things. Courage is simply a requirement of life."

TO A PLAYER WHOSE CAREER WAS FILLED WITH MANY CHALLENGING INJURIES:

"Good morning. Resist the temptation to ask 'why' too much. It is time to move on, super senior. There is much to be done. The best growth is ahead. Soon it will be time to really focus on US. I am so proud of you. I am thrilled your body has strengthened so much. You have an incredible opportunity now. You have earned every bit of what's ahead."

FOR TWO SPECIAL PLAYERS FIGHTING BACK FROM INJURY:

"It is okay to fail, okay to put yourself out there in a way to test your limits beyond what you have ever imagined. Having sheer bravery and courage is so necessary for success in life. Assuming the risk of failure allows you great freedom in your pursuit of many things—freedom to take on challenges while holding back absolutely nothing. There are no promises, and dreaming big is the way to go, knowing full well that things may not go your way. That is the risk we all assume for greatness. This is much easier to write about than to actually do. But, then again, you are ready."

———————

I loved sharing morning wisdom with the team and individuals who needed a boost at various times. My background, with all my issues and experiences, carved out a niche for me to think broadly and with empathy. This is truly the best thing about coaching young people. Being a better coach, each day is the real trick.

After my episodes, I saw more clearly, and my improved skills of observation and listening allowed my empathy to grow for those who felt they wanted to share their story, whatever their story, as an aspiring elite athlete. After my experience of being named a bipolar individual, I have great admiration and empathy for anyone who has to hold back about who they are because of fear of external judgments.

I feel a kindred spirit with them. I am a person who had very similar experiences of fighting for privacy and acceptance from others. I was afraid of the backlash that could occur for me in my life, just as other women I coached had to cope with criticism and stigmas attached to them. I lived in fear of being "outed" inappropriately, and I had felt that sting on a few occasions. There were very few people I could trust. But, I was happiest around those I did trust, and who may have similar stories to share about feeling accepted and not being discriminated against due to a life situation beyond your control. I have enjoyed the company of strong, gay women who made the choice to live free for years, back when it was absolutely unaccepted. They have shared their own authentic lives for years. Only after I was diagnosed and accepted my situation, and healed from all the events that occurred, could I publicly talk about my life as a bipolar mother, wife, coach, and mentor. Perhaps I was becoming a bit more comfortable in my own skin. Here are simple, but poignant, words from one of my favorite books, "The Velveteen Rabbit":

"You become. It takes a long time. That's why it doesn't happen often to people who break easily, or have sharp edges, or who have to be carefully kept. Generally, by the time you are Real, most of your hair has been loved off, and your eyes drop out and you get loose in the joints and very shabby. But these things don't matter at all, because once you are Real, you can't be ugly, except to people that don't understand."

———————

Back in the day, a wonderful fan at Maine used to send me letters of support on occasion. I can still remember her name: Lucille Dostie. In every note she would always be so kind, and closed each one of her heartfelt letters with "please don't overdue." These letters began arriving after my first episode. I smiled when they arrived, but in reality, it took quite some time to appreciate what she was trying to tell me. I still felt that I could push further in trying to be that person who could do all things, and I often forgot to say no. After having Maddie—returning to work the very next day from home and within the week to the office, pumping milk to simplify the breast-feeding process with efficiency, running a practice, coaching a very memorable season with the team as we headed to the NCAA Tournament, and accepting a coaching position to take a team overseas to Belgium following the season—I cannot say I was thinking about overdue at the time. I was so proud of myself to take on that "strong woman" role and show that it all could be done.

I think back to a great conversation with my early mentor, Coach Joe, when discussing being a mom and a head coach. As a former coach at West Point and then Auburn, he is a terrific motivator. He challenged me and indicated it might not be possible for me to balance life as a mom and a coach. We always talked about working by objectives as a twenty-four-hour process, seven days a week. I enjoyed my lunchtime runs with Joe. He always made me think. I was bound and determined to show him that I had what it takes to carry out all the responsibilities of the profession. The "I can do it all" spirit was ingrained in my young brain and gave me a great sense of purpose.

I also was not a great listener at the time. My family and close friends sometimes would caution me, especially after Maddie's birth. As a former high school All-American ball player, and a solid guard at the Division I level of collegiate sports, I just knew I had the endurance to push through, regardless of the wisdom to the contrary and despite the toll the schedule was taking on me. For any person, the challenge of the early coaching rigors and schedule can prove to be daunting indeed. For me and those around me, as a person with a genetic component traced to bipolar disorder, the costs turned out to be quite high.

What would I tell my young self today? First and foremost, as a young person in a new job, manage your enthusiasm properly. Of course, you want to do each and every thing to forward your team or company. Having children can be a beautiful thing as those little ones have a way of keeping life in perspective. But, the secret is learning how to say "yes" and how to say "no." A coach can be a great messenger of principles and motivation. I was asked to speak all over the state of Maine during my time coaching there. I took great pride in saying "yes" to all of the invitations, despite my already packed schedule and my need to have quiet time with my daughter and husband. You want to just focus and go, go, go onto the next event. But try to pace yourself, young aspiring coach. Do not be so intent on building something great in a day or week or a month.

Pause. Learn how to be still. See the beauty of life and the gorgeous fall colors in the neighborhood where you live. Be intense, but smile more and take time to hear the stories from family, the players or other folks in your life at the time. Stay incredibly organized to help the rhythm of the day. It is not a matter of having to do certain things the same way, or at the same time every day, but it is a matter of supporting yourself to dress easily in the morning, eat well, and find time for exercise. Limit your complications in all ways. Enjoy going to bed early after a hot bath. Slow down enough to regroup. Rely on others and learn to delegate. Trust your supporting cast and challenge them to rise. Set the tone and set the philosophy, but allow others to work in concert with you. Sit back and understand the human dimension of people and projects. Fear of failure helps churn the motivational wheels, but sometimes those wheels can spin too fast and burn out far too quickly.

Build your sense of belonging with others. Understand the value of community. Build that base with care by reaching out and being proactive with people and relationships. Make sense of things intellectually. Slow down and think through the process. Trust your work and trust others. Rather than thinking of outcomes and championships all the time, work on building memories with all those around you, and certainly for your team or organization. Make those gestures that connect by making a phone call or sending a written note. Seek valor.

Valor is a word that may not be used widely. But understanding its dual meaning requires a sense of perspective and allows one to remind oneself what is most important.

"Valor is the word where courage, and the ability to overcome fear, combine with doing the honorable thing," US Army General (Ret.) Martin Dempsey once shared on a Zoom with the Duke athletic department. His definition has always made me pause, and think deeply.

CLIMBING MOUNTAINS

Mental health combines two great words that are both positive in nature. Despite all the diseases that exist today, it is the diseases of despair than can shorten life expectancy in our country today. Many people are dying from helplessness, or a lack of help and understanding. When we talk about getting good sleep, taking our medications, being careful with consumption of alcohol, and regular visits with our doctors, it all seems so simple. There is a true grieving process that takes place as a person is diagnosed with any serious disease. The road to recovery is marked by denial, anger, bargaining, depression and finally, acceptance. There is no skipping past the traditional stages of grief and recovery. It is hard to cut short any of these stages. Catching people as they move through these stages is critical. The depression phase is the most dangerous. Our world has to cope with our "new normal" awaiting us.

Loyalty to one's mind is a most cherished attribute. It is highly fulfilling and life-changing to find the evolving, educated, emancipating, and erudite possibilities beyond an illness. The extraordinary equilibrium comes first, and the quiet liberation follows. However, the challenges are grand and imperfect. The unquiet mind is not always loose and damaging. It can hover and move in gentle spaces, but the inconsequential details of life can be terribly boring. Therein lies the danger of its significance.

The common mind just does not always fill the vast space of ideas and creativity so craved and revealed while a person is in a manic state. Those with bipolar disorder learn this reality, and sometimes choose to go off their meds to seek the magnificence of the manic mind's power to generate astounding thoughts and work.

Going rogue is an interesting concept. It can be manufactured by poor choices like not staying committed to meds, or it can just be a state of being within the mental health world. Those with impaired mental health are, not by choice, truly rogue in a unique way. The impairment sneaks up on you without giving you a chance to prepare. Suddenly, you are an outlier, looking in from afar, and feeling alone in your new space. When elephants go rogue, they leave the herd with intention. They choose a dangerous way of living. With mental health impairment, there is no intention. You are simply ambushed. You cannot defend yourself. There is an enormous sense of loneliness that permeates the whole process, from diagnosis to recovery. This is a dangerous time where "escape" methods can be developed.

Then, there are the faces—the faces of your loved ones or anyone who learns about your reality in its entirety. There is a raw fear of your unknown, although bravery to handle the eyes of others grows through time, and certainly through sports. Faith over fear is a daily focus point in competition, and in living under the gaze of others. Contentment training is a challenging process. It is learned through the wide range of suffering. This suffering can catapult you forward to a new reality beyond what you could ever imagine. This positive, relentless, and fierce attitude must be cultivated. Of course, this is much easier to describe than to execute daily.

Bravery, courage and perspective are needed through friendship, support, and others' stories that foster strength and resilience within your mind. As a mood disorder person, I am constantly looking for books with stories of gigantic leaps of faith and inspiration. A dear friend of mine, and a vigorous person who has climbed most peaks in the Himalayas and travelled the world as an adventurer with scuba diving expeditions as well, suggested one of the denser books I have ever attempted to read, "The Snow Leopard" by Peter Matthiessen.

The infamous snow leopard is rarely seen, yet climbers pursue the fantastic challenge to see one while experiencing all the natural elements. This animal is something so elusive: pure white in the winter, and a simple brown in all other seasons. How is it this rare animal can change its color to fit within its natural world? It adapts. It evolves for maximum safety and survival. Those mountain climbers strip themselves of everything and expose their total selves.So, my motivation to write, complete, and publish this book began with the thought that we all have more to share, know and discover within our own experiences. I feel as if I have been stripped down a bit through my experience with a mood disorder, working over the multiple peaks, just like the Annapurna in Nepal.

Special friends, with full lives and interesting stories, have a way of sharing perspectives so subtly. A quiet lunch conversation, followed up through descriptions via text or otherwise, reaches out in unique ways. My dear friend, Sally Vamvakias, has climbed almost every peak worldwide except Mount Everest. Her experiences, wisdom, and courage cannot be aptly explained here as it would take a longer book! However, her words lead us through the eyes of challenge, whatever mountain we may be climbing.

"All climbers do not summit every mountain. There can be the death zones where the individual is not functioning at a high cognitive level. Only living in the present, and being completely aware of yourself, allows you to unpeel the truth. Your mind can be unsafe for now—on the mountain—and you can still find peace for yourself. Once you have pushed past your doubts, through each step, your mind becomes crystal clear, and you know that your mind is not going back to where it was."

Exploring is a method of grounding. We, too, have to find our space in this comfort of peace, and of knowing that we can make it through. We must get past the idea to "clutch the mountain," clinging to the tightness of fear that, on the mountain and in life, can get people killed. How much does it take to be full in a life? How will I know when it's enough? I chose, and I hope many choose, to abandon a sense of security, to push past the clutch, and to accept what comes with it as a condition of doing it.

What is on the other side of these mountains of doubt that we face? What exactly is normal? It is okay to see the dark before the light is clear. Sometimes you must go exploring beyond the comforts in your life currently. It is okay. Your world is special, and you are gifted once you dare to find the truth.

Sally V and her life serve as a great inspiration to me. Her seemingly simple gesture of sharing stories and a great book brought me to a whole new space of thinking. Both Mainers, we share a common bond and love for all things natural and simple. Maine is such a small state in terms of population; everyone seems to know each other. All of us get lost in the peaks and valleys of life. Whether it is mental health or sports, the metaphor is long-lasting. Each mountaineer has a singular focus: simply, the next step right in front of them. The steps can feel endless, and the peaks and valleys are too numerous to fathom all together. So, we break things down to parts, small steps each day, each getting us closer to the freedoms we seek.

Finding that freedom and reaching the other side of the mountains we climb takes mental balance. Combined with a keen sense of trust, balance allows us to navigate relationships in the healthiest manner. This must be worked on daily. It takes courage to share and self-deprecate while keeping a sense of humor, too. Fellow bipolar folks are a great source of strength for one another. The stories and inside jokes of our mad existence are helpful, and often are laced with humorous anecdotes for what we share. People make relationships. Relationships do not make people. Any shared relationship where authenticity prevails lends itself to the deepest connections, and the most fun as well.

It has been a process to learn to surrender to faith and

events beyond my control. I learned the clear difference between surrendering and succumbing: the word "surrender" can connote weakness and giving up. But in the world of mental health recovery and growth, to surrender is to be brave and admirable. It is not succumbing in a weak-minded way. It is not about competition, losing or winning. It is noble, forgiving, and free. It is valor in every sense of the word.

Emotional balance drives success for all professions, in business, or in life at home. Preparation and patience are constant ingredients. Coaching young people requires the understanding and gratification that they need time and a chance to grow. Growth is understood in small increments. The scoreboard is not the focus. But staying in the game is. You try and you try again. Each failure gets you to the next breakthrough. Just as in golf psychology, each bad shot is a setup for a great shot.

Sports are a metaphor for life. Sports and love of our craft can prepare us for anything.

We endure long hours of dedication and commitment to achieve ultimate successes. We all deserve the ultimate brain to accompany the incredible skills that student-athletes and all athletes exhibit in their respective sports. The ultimate example of valor can be seen when we can modify and change our brain chemistry to serve us better in our craft. We are brave. We are filled with courage. Let those concepts apply to every aspect of each challenge that comes our way. Even the challenges that are unwelcome and arrive without permission are a part of the game of competition.

The lessons learned can be long-term and change the fabric of our thinking regarding many different aspects of our lives. We all have a chance to make a difference. Mental health in its grandest form, and in its challenged state of sickness, can be a huge benefit for all. The shoring up of our collective ability to be there for folks working through such issues is critical. My heart aches for those who struggle with a mental health diagnosis, and those who may follow.

There are so many triggers lurking. Those triggers can ignite a long list of actions that can exacerbate the already daunting problems of the day. Action is the key word for us all. So is perseverance, as we take each step toward the summit of acceptance and freedom.

Sharing stories of our journeys—failures and successes—is part of the long continuum of learning and coping with mental disease. As you can see through my ordeal, it takes a collective approach to find the keys to unlock the high functioning brain. We all deserve the best brain space and balance for a lifetime, but we must climb step-by-step toward it.

As Viktor Frankel shared in "Man's Search for Meaning," ". . . in terms of grave suffering, some can brutalize others as a result of the suffering, some give up, but those who focus on a reference point beyond this world can overcome even the worst form of suffering."

Hope, education, and awareness, combined with motivating change from those involved, are the keys to unlimited growth. If one life can be saved in any circumstance in the world, by all the medical efforts, dialogue, education, training, and motivation to find truth, then we have become more advanced and will save lives. If we succeed, and live without the limitation of stigmas and fear, we all, despite any challenges in our lives, can truly be free. We can all get to the other side of the mountain.

NEWFOUND FAITH

I t was a beautiful Maine morning: August 9, 2019. The sun was just peeking over the smooth and silky Maine ocean. The hue of the morning sunrise was yellow, and expansive across the glassy water. I practically skipped to the shoreline to watch the sun rising so mystically. I was fifty-three years old and ready to plunge into a new journey. A sense of peace, and gentle excitement, permeated my thoughts.

My sister Carolyn and brother-in-law Brian were walking toward the water's edge. Their three beautiful children soon followed. The place for this new journey had been chosen carefully: the ocean, alongside a special home where Brian had long talked to me about faith in his life. I was not accustomed to such conversations as I had grown up as a rarely-practicing Catholic. I remember that the highlight of going to Sunday service was going to McDonald's after mass with my brother and sister, led by my dad. I loved those McDonald's pancakes! We did not attend mass often, and after a while we did not go at all.

―――――――――――

My faith journey came about slowly. I always thought God was good for other people who needed Him, but because I was not raised with much formal religion, my spiritual faith in life and nature was good enough for me. I have always had that spiritual side of looking up to the heavens, wondering about all the special people in my life who have passed on. Most of us do this, I think, regardless of our religious beliefs. The universe is fascinating, and I have always believed in a higher power.

But then, in the fall of my second season at Duke, a dark, round mole on my forehead was diagnosed as a malignant melanoma. My mom and sis had always been pushing me to get it looked at, even in my MSU days, but I was always too busy and also thought it was a natural part of me, so their approach always seemed a bit vain. With all sorts of folks changing their looks and faces, I thought the spot was a signature kind of thing for me. Not exactly. Two surgeries on my forehead later, with stitches that made me look like Frankenstein's monster, I can remember seeing Coach K at our adjacent parking spaces: he saw me getting out of the car and took one look and said, "What happened to the other guy?" Great comment, as I had felt very uncomfortable returning to work with my black-and-blue eyes and cross-stitched forehead. It gave me a laugh and a better thought heading into the office. Soon I was on my way to healing. It was in the fall and it only cost me a few days on the couch, and then I was back to normal. This started a long journey through lots of cutting and scars to remove possible malignant cells that could manifest into something much worse, like my first real melanoma.

Then I prayed a great deal to the heavens and to God, too. Privately, I was very scared and wondered if this could be the thing that would take my life. I prayed for myself and my family to heal permanently, and to have the threatening cells stop. I had to get checked each month. It was a constant reminder of the virtues of living, but also of events outside our control that can tear at the fabric of your mind and body. For a while, it was shots and cutting and stitches almost every time I went—eight, to be exact. My assistant Bobby always cringed when I went for another appointment. The stitches and scars looked intimidating and were very unattractive. They are my warrior scars to this day. I actually coached in a game after a larger problematic area that had developed on my neck was removed. It ended with quite a scar, but the stitches were fresh that day. I took some painkillers so I could coach, but I did not realize I could only turn my head one way without the stitches feeling like razor blades cutting into my skin. I really should not have coached that day. We lost that game and I am sure I was not at my best.

After that time, my beliefs slowly started to change. *Who was I praying to?* I must truly believe in God to ask Him for so much healing. Maybe all of my friends who led lives with faith had something extra, something that could strengthen me? I was much more open, but still not all the way there. It took some rough injury-laden seasons—with multiple and repeat knee surgeries to our players, and a couple of tough seasons, and a few folks to question my intentions and leadership—to push me further into the world of faith, morning pages, and devotionals. Eventually, church was a great thing for me, as my friend Ellie Hoover led the way. One thing is true and a tribute to Duke and the women's program: many people wanted my job and were not afraid to politic for it. It was interesting at the time, and challenging, but being able to compartmentalize is a huge key for all coaches. With a new faith becoming stronger each day, my morning time became valuable and very enjoyable.

Later, when my kidneys were struggling to keep pace with me, and kidney disease was a real threat given my medication adjustments, my strength grew even more as I prayed for health and a recovery of my kidney function which seemed unlikely. And things worked out very well as my health got back to normal. I had been fatigued a great deal during the kidney challenges, but I did coach throughout the ordeal, and our team had a great run in Athens, Georgia that year in the NCAA tourney fighting to that Sweet 16. My faith continued to grow, and I found room for my devotionals each morning and connected with some of my players at a higher level. I loved sharing my *Morning Shares* with the team or individual players at various times. These women were Christians, and welcomed the thoughts and care.

Leaving Duke, followed by another cancer scare, and then a full-blown hysterectomy at age fifty-five, has a way of bringing your faith further along. Faith is a good day/bad day commitment, but these events were coming at a rapid-fire pace all in the same year, and within months of each other. Twelve weeks of non-exercise recovery is quite a challenge for a person who enjoys working out five or six days a week, and I love exercise to clear my mind and keep great brain health.

And then my dad died. Later, with the covid virus in full swing, my father, Capt. Robert Palombo, a terrific naval aviator, passed rather suddenly despite his eighty-two years. My family was one of those looking in the window during his last hours. With covid and all the horrible events that have occurred, prayer has been so necessary to coping. I am still coping with my father's passing at this writing. I believe, when it comes to our parents, we always will keep coping.

———————————————

My full conversion to my newfound faith came at the hands of Pastor Rob, Brian's dear friend. He had agreed to baptize me in the ocean in Maine at the home of my brother-in-law Brian and my sister Carolyn. The night before, we had much discussion about faith and this commitment to being baptized. Bible verses and prayer and stories of faith were all a part of the evening, even after much discussion about life and faith the evening before. Christine and James, Brian's sister and brother in-law, had agreed to come enjoy the conversion with us. It was a very thoughtful and stimulating evening, great preparation for the next morning, and overwhelming at times, too. I was new to this whole experience, and a bit amazed by my lack of knowledge or any command of the Bible. Pastor Rob had talked on the phone to my Pastor Clay to bless the baptism. Rob's wife Sim was also there. I felt supported and ready for the new journey. I wore a comfortable long-sleeved white top and shorts. The sensitive reflection of light from the water brought a sense of purity to the occasion. The light white top seemed to fit in perfectly. The water temperature was typical of a Maine August—a bit warmer than usual, due to the time of year, but still icy and hearty, as we Mainers have become accustomed to while growing up in such a state of beauty, and natural wonders, and the often-freezing Atlantic Ocean. The warmth of the day and the peace of the water created a serene environment.

My own family was back in Durham, North Carolina, but I had rented a house in Maine to spend time with my dear parents and my sister's family. I often spend time in Maine in August, alone first, and then with the family joining in. I wanted to be alone for this step of faith. The baptism was a very personal time for me. I was eager to share all the details later, but for now, I was simply me and, in my mind, free and moving forward past all the scares and fears in my life, preparing for all the challenges to come.

On my baptism day, Pastor Rob and I carefully stepped into the chilly water, around and on the rocks, as we moved out to where we were waist-deep. The shock of entering the clear, cold, and green water was certainly familiar. Seaweed squished under my feet. I had a steady balance, and then Rob began the words of God's grace. I listened carefully, and repeated each word calmly and with a clear voice. He was gentle and strong as he dipped me backwards into the water. I sprang up with a great sense of joy, nervous in a way, and certainly feeling refreshed. There were claps and quiet shouts from those of my family present. I felt morning glory without a doubt, and a renewed sense of peace, hope, and responsibility.

So many special individuals in my life were a part of that day without even needing to be present. I am grateful to each one of them for their friendship and willingness to share their stories of faith. Sometimes the stories took longer to tell, but the wait was well worth it. As a person with a mood disorder for life, I am allowing faith to become much more central in my life. God bless those folks who helped me arrive to this space. It has been quite a journey.

My unknown journey began through a long line of friendships

and grace. All my life I have worked hard to choose my friends carefully—certainly a good way to live for all. I have been truly blessed, but have often been unaware of the possibilities before me with all my Sisters and Brothers in Christ (SICs and BICs) who have developed and had grown naturally and somewhat serendipitously over twenty years or more.

It all started in the great state of Michigan, and continued through our move to our special home state of North Carolina. Joanie, a dear friend and neighbor in East Lansing, Michigan, befriended our family literally on the first day of our arrival there. The introduction meeting took place at the infamous Great Apple Bagel. We were sitting and enjoying our breakfast as Joanie walked in with what seemed like a parade of too many kids. Joanie and Eric are the proud parents of ten beautiful children. There was an offer to dinner quickly. We were thrilled for Joanie's immediate Midwestern hospitality. We enjoyed a wonderful dinner with everyone.

The prayer we shared before the meal struck me as thoughtful and a nice gesture of friendship. Of course, I had rarely prayed in my life. It seemed like something that other people did. However, I said truly my first *amen* on that eve. Then, without hesitation, our new life began in East Lansing—seven great years of up, up and away in terms of family growth and team success.

Joanie became a most special friend during those times. I loved that she knew little about my work, and coaching, so our conversations centered around family, and all the activities Maddie would share with Joanie's eldest daughter, Natalie Rose. Joanie exposed me to her religious beliefs, and there were more prayers shared along the way. Still, I never felt compelled to examine faith in my life. Many years would pass before I ever really understood.

In East Lansing we felt a tremendous sense of the neighborly welcome. John had met a great guy, an AAU coach, when he first flew to East Lansing to find our new house. I was unable to join him right away due to giving birth to Jack, and I stayed at home with him for a quiet month, before all the Spartan excitement began. But John and his dear friend Stan were quite capable house hunters, and they were able to buy a house and fit in a round of golf on the same day.

Nate, Pat, and his family became special supporters of our program and team. Nate became our Director of Basketball Operations and played a huge role when we made our Final Four run in 2005. Nate spoke regularly of his mentoring of youth, and his faith. I thought this was very interesting, but again kept my laser focus on developing our team while raising a family in a new environment. He was a great friend no doubt, but we kept our work and personal issues separate, and talked only about working with so many great student-athletes at Michigan State. I was not familiar with his faith walk, and though we never talked about it, he sensed in our conversations that something was always there. I remember vividly, after he began working with me at Michigan State, the day I made a comment that indicated my general view of faith:

"I'm not religious, but I do believe in a higher power."

Over the years, especially after I left Michigan State, our conversations became more reflective about my innermost thoughts. Nate enjoyed visiting us at Duke, and having time to come to practice to see the team. Nate noticed, in particular, that some of the players were talking about their faith openly. Nate and Kyra exchanged words and thoughts regarding their own faith stories. I supported all, while leaning on Nate to teach me further. Nate and I encouraged the team to create a voluntary group for devotional time. Months later, a defining moment occurred when I visited Nate at the hospital. I knew something was missing in my life. Nate and I shared some of my feelings and thoughts about God, and we prayed. At that moment and afterwards, I began to be more comfortable with my faith, and I took another step toward God.

Rene was one of our special players at MSU. Rene could help explain my words of motivation, and action, to the team. It is always good to have those players who can add to clarity of thinking for the others. In this way, Rene was a leader and interpreter. I felt a warmth and a kindred spirit with her and her family almost immediately during the recruiting process. She was a low-maintenance recruit with a very positive outlook. She often explained me to others as an intense coach, bound and determined to help the team rise to the highest level. I was a young coach still, and wanted so much to succeed in my first Power Five conference. Rene was the spiritual leader of her team. She spoke calmly and with great poise. She listened and nurtured her teammates to listen as well, and learn each step of the way through all the challenges a season can bring. She also was ferocious on defense and loved to attack "off the bounce." She became a critical starter and sixth player during her career.

She was a huge key to our special run in 2005. She made game-winners. One of her best moments was putting in a winning shot by grabbing a loose ball on a scramble on the floor, with time running out on the clock. She made the top ten in ESPN highlights, and more importantly, sent our team to the first Sweet Sixteen in school history, with dreams of a national championship going further. Only years later would I appreciate Rene and her upbringing in a family truly dedicated to faith. Later, Rene became an assistant coach with me at Duke for four years. She grew as a coach, and continued to offer leadership on and off the court, while sharing her faith with all the Duke women she served. Rene is a truth teller, faith leader, and great mentor to all those around her.

―――――――――――――

After Michigan, arriving at Duke was awkward for me, at times, because we had made such a tough move for our thirteen-year-old daughter, Maddie. She was taken from so much love and security, not to mention a state title for her basketball team, since she would have played for East Lansing High School, a very strong program. East Lansing High School ended up winning a title without Maddie. As Mom, I needed support on and off the court during the ups and downs of the family transitioning. Taking the lead of Duke's program that had already earned great success prior to our arrival was a challenge. There was a very small margin of gaining more success—a national championship.

Mitch was a leader, mentor, and chaplain at Duke for the football team. He had a keen interest in mentoring young people in their development and their faith. With his University of Tennessee background, he loved and appreciated women's basketball. Soon he began counseling with some of our players coping with adversity, and all the challenges that being an elite level athlete brings. In a short period of time, he became a dear friend and supporter for me to bounce ideas off, and discuss the life of coaching with all its joy and challenges. Mitch is a person of great faith. He became our team chaplain, and gave the most incredibly motivating talks during our pregame meals. His prayers were always spot-on and reflective of our team's growth. I loved to hear his booming voice. He could make us laugh, so we absorbed his powerful message with ease. He always ended with very uplifting and positive thoughts, and finished with a personal team prayer, directed to all of us. We all loved having him on our side.

I tried to have lunch with him once a week where we covered all topics in life. Over the years, we shared many laughs and a lot of Chinese food at our favorite spot. He always prayed before the meal. I found it comforting, but still I was reluctant to pursue a more detailed commitment to sharing faith because I was often moving forward at a breakneck pace to keep the program progressing. He coaxed me to think about faith, and often told me I had to learn "to be still" and "pause" throughout the stresses on and off the court. We laughed a lot. I cried, too. He never cried! I still was reluctant to examine faith any further. Brother Mitch still did not flinch, and continued to walk the word around me.

We had great conversations about "Who is God?" and "What He is doing?" Ironically, it was after Mitch left Duke when I truly began to understand what God might be all about in a much broader context, as Mitch later said to me with his big smile, and his very natural and appealing sense of humor:

"You know that I was supposed to be the one to hold you under the water to baptize you! I am blessed to call you my friend, but most importantly, my sister in Christ."

My relationship with Rishal reflects the fact that college teammates can be lifelong friends, well after the ball stops bouncing. Reconnecting can come in various forms and opportunities. Rishal and I found a way to reconnect almost twenty-five years after our time together at Northwestern University. We had been competitive and fun teammates. We shared a closeness in college, but not much more than the usual team experiences, and sometimes trouble, that we managed to cultivate. Ah, that growing time of college life. We all love Rishal so much. She brought much joy and a positive attitude to all things. I knew she was special, but I could not put a finger on that something extra.

Only later, as I was moving toward faith in Durham, did I feel and witness her faith and ability to "share the word" with such clarity and motivation. The melanoma had appeared, the day-to-day challenges at Duke continued, and later my kidney issue had surfaced, all while growing a family and working to find the right balance in my life. Rishal was always just a phone call away.

She began to share her faith more openly as I asked a lot of rookie questions. I found a way to see her occasionally because we often recruited in the Atlanta area. She loved the game and took the time to sit with me as we, together, had fun evaluating talent. She was always interested in the spirit of the student-athlete. She looked for more, for the intangible pieces that reveal character. Great times were had over a lunch or two throughout my Duke days. She also gently encouraged me to explore faith in my life. I was listening, but moving at a slower pace. Rishal has become one of my most dear friends, and a true SIC in every sense of the word.

A favorite memory that Rishal shared with me exemplifies how she and I both enjoy looking for God's work and celebrating it accordingly. Rishal had helped me study the word, and showed me how to bring prayer into my daily life. She liked to say that I had "become a sponge with a heart for Him." She likened my motivation to a book she enjoyed, "The God Chasers," by Tom Tenney. She loved this book, and shared with me that it had been a part of her experience and spiritual awakening.

Rishal frequented many of our games at Duke and became aware of the players, and their stories. She had watched Kyra, our point guard, endure so much pain from knee injuries throughout her career. Rishal was there when Kyra returned from her injuries to play in her first game. After two years watching from the sidelines, Kyra amazingly hit an eighty-four-foot shot on that very first game back. Rishal always sees the "God winks," as she calls them. Her radiant smile would say that Kyra was just getting "her sign, anointing, and favor" that all was going to be okay for her, and for her courageous return to the game she loves so dearly.

Rishal was a firm believer in our team's amazing comeback season in my final year at Duke. She would always remind me about God's path, and there was no stopping us from going from tenth place to third in the very challenging Atlantic Coast Conference. She was a believer long before there was evidence of our success. She delighted and prayed for us often during our eleven-game winning streak which catapulted us to just a few points away from second and almost first place in the league. Rishal's smile and beautiful faith can change the dynamics of any room or situation. When all the good things started to happen for that special team, she just would smile and say, "Josey, I told you so. God is growing in you and your team, and girl, ya'll better watch out."

Sometimes you can leave a place where friendships begin, and continue to evolve well beyond distance and life changes. Melissa and Dan were good friends and supporters during my career at MSU. Both busy doctors with a beautiful family, they still found a way to support the Michigan State program. We enjoyed many great moments together, but saw each other very little as we were all caught up in raising our children and finding ourselves immersed in our challenging careers. After we had already been in Durham over ten years, and as we started to text-message more from afar to keep in touch, Melissa began to share her faith with me. She learned of my growing interest and took the time to send books of faith that I could read in the morning. Melissa always smiled and joked that I was one of the most intellectual people she had ever met—these were choice words coming from a super doc with many accolades to her name. She remarked that I analyze and question everything: I suppose it is the coach mind trying to find my way. Her positive and uplifting words make me feel good.

I often sit in our screened-in porch, waiting to welcome the sunrise. I love my morning time and enjoy trying to learn more, and reach out each morning with a family share discovered in the daily messages of the Word. Melissa and I would share stories and prayer over the many events and happenings in our lives. Her song of the day texts are truly my most favorite shares by far. Melissa literally built my faith song list to almost one hundred great songs, and it's still counting.

My shares were also sent to the players on the team who I knew had faith as a part of their lives. Then I just decided to send all shares to everyone on the team, without regard to their faith level. I asked them all directly if they liked the faith outreach. Their enthusiastic "yes" was eye-opening for me. I chose to share the word and the amazing songs, as we dealt with great success and very tough times, too. I have over three years' worth of notes and thoughts I accumulated through the verses, and lessons, in the devotional books. I found that I was leaving a trail of thoughts for my family, players, and staff that had made me feel more whole, and allowed me as a parent, coach, and mentor to be better and to reach everyone at a deeper, and more interesting level.

———————

It's interesting to me that I started my career following the lead of my mentor, Joe. As I learned from him, I observed how we, the team and staff, would kneel for a team prayer as we gathered around him immediately after his pregame talk. That prayer stayed in my head all through my Maine years, my Michigan State days, and for most of my Duke career as well. I actually led the prayer through memory and belief in it, not really knowing what "it" was about:

"Lord, let us have the power, courage, and character to play forty minutes of Duke basketball... Michigan State basketball ... Maine basketball. Amen."

I added the "character" word to give a bit of myself to the prayer. It seemed like the right thing to do. Joe had introduced the prayer to me during my time at Auburn. I had no hesitation in using it, even without really understanding the overall concepts of organized faith. All my players accepted it, and appeared to appreciate the pregame ritual. Like me, many did not have organized faith in their lives, but it connected while providing a much higher level of togetherness and motivation. In my last few years at Duke, as I became stronger and more confident in my faith, I decided to change the prayer. I felt differently about the words after my baptism—prayer thoughts and word choices came to me more easily, and gave me a sense of independence in my newfound faith.

"Heavenly Father, let us celebrate our gifts, get better together, and have fun playing off each other for forty minutes or whatever it takes. Amen."

This prayer developed after I had given the responsibility to Kyra, one of our players of great faith, who delivered the team prayer the year she was recovering from her very challenging knee injuries. After her recovery, she passed the torch to me. She was back, and ready to compete, and she said she would appreciate the prayer given by me. I was touched, willing, and grateful, while recognizing I was beginning to lead in a more committed, faithful way. My faith was growing in all sorts of spaces.

Prayers, growth and change happened, but how did I ever get to church? My tennis doubles partner, Ellie, had become a great friend through all of our wild days of competitive and aggressive tennis. We both love to play, and we played off each other very well. I was a novice tennis player when we moved to Durham. I first got my son Jack involved, and thoroughly enjoyed watching his lessons. Then Rebecca, the teaching pro, prodded me to play, but I was always concerned about my bad back. I did not understand the value of a clay court, with its softness and give to the body. When I started to play, I was a beginner moving through the rankings, as I observed other women of 4.0 and 4.5 status. These are USTA rankings that mark the players' competitive level, success, and experience. As a competitor, I knew I wanted to play at that high level, after starting at a 2.5 with that group of women. Ellie, of course, was already in that group.

After a few years, Ellie and I became a good match for USTA tennis competition. Playing was is an incredible release from coaching, and I felt how it made me better and more clear-thinking. I also found a dear and fun friend. I kept bugging Ellie to set up practice matches on Sundays. She would always look at me and wonder why I didn't understand that she goes to church on Sunday, and why in the world do I keep asking her for Sunday tennis? She is a direct person with a great sense of humor and peace. She had dealt with many exceedingly difficult health issues within her own family, and in her own life. She is a strong person of great character, and always lets everyone know exactly what she is thinking.

Finally, one day, in her usual sardonic and humorous manner, she reiterated that she would be in church again on Sunday, and asked me to stop requesting for that time with her. My response this time was, "Maybe I should just go with you?" She retorted quickly, with her wry and timely sense of humor, "I think that's a great idea. Lord knows you need it!" Off we went, tennis partners, dear friends, and newly found Sisters in Christ—an extraordinary combination indeed!

Ellie is proud that I have become a Christian. She often remarks that I have the same intense approach with faith as I have with coaching. She reminds me, and teases me about how I tend to absorb sermons at church, take copious notes, and try not to miss a thing. I appreciate that Ellie views me as much more than just a basketball coach. She often remarks, "God is going to use you, just you wait and see!" She keeps her sense of humor always as she has said, "Even though you have God's love with you, it sometimes does not seem that way on the tennis courts."

———————

A woman of great faith whom I observed as I was preparing to marry John was my mother-in-law, Eleanor "Queenie" McCallie. Back then, I was bereft of any kind of organized thought or faith. I can remember sitting in the McCallie kitchen during a visit to Chattanooga, Tennessee, as Mom McCallie prepared another great meal. She would listen to religious programs, and beautiful Christian songs, while she cooked up some of the best Southern food I have ever enjoyed. She did ask me about my faith, as John's father did. At first, I was intimidated. But Mom McCallie was very patient, and just let me be, to find my own way. There was no judging or pushing to make me a Christian before I married John. She was gentle, loving, and always asking others about their lives and stories. She used the word "appreciate" as much as any person I had ever known in my life. I always thought it was a wonderful grace note that Eleanor, my dear friend and tennis pal, shared the same first name as Eleanor "Queenie" McCallie. Two Eleanors, years apart in my life, had both made a profound influence in my life. I have always believed that Mom McCallie is looking down from the heavens, smiling widely about all these connections and developments in my life.

FAITHFUL PLAYERS

Just as her name implies, Faith Suggs was one of the most remarkable young women and student-athletes I ever recruited to Duke. Her history is quite heartwarming. As her dear mother, Susan, battled hard with melanoma, Faith had to carry on, with her father and brother, as the strong woman in the house at a very young age: she was only thirteen when her mother passed. I cannot fathom the pain for her family during those times.

Faith and I did not discuss faith directly during the time I coached her at Duke. Her energy and faith surrounded her as she carried herself with grace, and led the team in so many ways. She was pivotal to one of our Sweet Sixteen runs as we battled hard in Athens, Georgia for the first round of the NCAA tournament, the Sweet Sixteen, and then found our way to face Connecticut for a chance to advance to the Elite Eight. She was an unsung hero throughout her time at Duke. She was often called "the mother of the team."

Faith and I enjoyed many thoughtful conversations together. She expressed interest in my growing faith, and she said later that it was "raw and vulnerable" in a way where she could relate. As Faith recalled, "We were having a normal conversation, as we often did before practice, and Coach P said, 'You will share your story when you are ready to share your story.'" She would have the opportunity to educate others about the awful disease of melanoma.

Player-coach relationships go well beyond the court, and it

always amazing how that orange ball brings us together beyond the game.

Faith's father was very open and honest during the recruiting process. He and I enjoyed our conversations, and I found the whole family a joy to recruit. One evening, during one of our many phone calls, her dad came right out and asked me if I was bipolar. I was shocked by his question, yet he was sincere, and was wondering because of some information he had heard through the recruiting grapevine.

Recruiting is a tough business. Some coaches will use any rumor or gossip to gain an edge. As my heart sank with my wonderment of his question, I quickly found a way to respond to him: "Aren't all coaches a little bit bipolar, relative to the nature of the job?" He paused as he smiled through the phone and accepted my answer, and we moved forward in the conversation. I was caught off guard for sure, but was also very comfortable with Shafer Suggs. The conversation moved on smoothly as we talked about Faith coming to Duke.

I have always believed there must be a few other bipolar coaches out there in the world. The demands of the work, the constant ups and downs of winning and losing, the scrutiny from the media, and impatient fans, can all trigger events that may lead to such a mood disorder situationally or chemically, or both. I hope and pray that they are not undiagnosed. The world is a very lonely place for those who have not sought out and found the right support for brain health. Of course, there are many mood disorders that can affect coaches and student-athletes.

Faith and her family made me question my own faith because of the unfathomable loss of her mom. Faith was so strong and carried herself with such grace after such devastation. Her dad had also hit a nerve with his direct question. At the time, I was scared about his question. Who would know me that personally? How did he get that thought to ask me? How would folks use it against me, when they did not know facts, and the rumor just swirled? Did former assistants or administrators from back in my Maine days reveal this to other coaches and administrators along my professional path? My reaction was laced with fear. What might have been if I had faith earlier in my life to help me come to peace with my own story? Many times, I have thought about what could have been. We had enjoyed so much success at all the schools with all the players and staffs along the way. Reason does not always work in recruiting, as enthusiasm and emotion can take over any decision. I enjoyed those special recruits who found the balance between emotion and reason in their decision-making. Of course, part of true faith is trusting in God's path for you. I still remain scared and guarded. I was not ready for God and His path. Faith's family had struck a sensitive nerve in my life, but in a positive way. More thinking and wondering about my own journey followed.

On another positive note, it was a joy to organize the first of many melanoma-awareness games at Duke. Polka Dot Mama, in conjunction with the Melanoma Research Alliance and devoted organizers like Tracy C. and her team, worked very hard to help us bring public awareness of this insidious disease. Together, we all fought back with action, and faith for Faith.

Kyra Lambert was a point guard at Duke who dealt with incredible adversity as she fought her way back from three serious knee injuries. Her work ethic and determination to get back on the court was incredible. We lost her for further post-season play to a knee injury as we competed in the first round of the NCAA Tournament. It was a great game, and Kyra was a huge piece to our puzzle. In the first half, a player from the opposing team, off-balance and moving very aggressively, ran right into the side of Kyra's leg. It was an awful time as our team tried to adjust for the second half. We did win that first game handily. In the next game, playing without

Kyra, we lost our chance for the Sweet Sixteen, succumbing to a very young and talented Oregon team. Oregon, a few years later, went on to be a Final Four team, and thus a national championship contender.

Early in Kyra's career I was an ignorant non-faith coach. With my pregame prayer I was leading from the heart, but without knowing God's grace and support. As I observed Kyra, I could see how important faith was to her life and rehabilitation. She was strong and had no question she would play again. I admired her will to get through three knee surgeries with such a profound sense of strength. Soon we began to talk more about faith. My morning work had developed over time, and I felt comfortable to share the word with her. Kyra recognized that our last two years together included many more varied conversations, beyond just school, team, individual talk, and basketball thoughts.

"When Coach P started her spiritual journey, she was honest and humble in her approach. We shared many special moments of grace and its timing, but my favorite one throughout my time at Duke occurred in her office."

That day, I chose to share with Kyra that I had been baptized while in Maine. Her response was truly one of the most memorable moments between a coach and a player for me and my career off the court. Her eyes filled with tears, and she gave that big, wide-eyed Kyra smile. As she later shared with me, my choice to earnestly pursue my faith was one of her highlights and best remembrances from her Duke experience. Kyra and her strength, patience, openness, and conversation gave me the power to move forward. She, as point guards often do, led me there well beyond the parameters of the court, beyond her court vision, to a true and faithful vision for life.

———

Later in life, it is such a joy to find new friends from all kinds of experiences. Sally Vamvakias, my mountaineering friend, told me many stories about her worldwide travel. She spoke about the passing of her oldest daughter in a car accident, and how she went about coping and learning from such an enormous family trauma. I had known Sally from years ago during my Maine coaching days. Sally had served on the University of Maine board of governors, undertaking a myriad of amazing projects. She was always so active, statewide, in forwarding causes and raising dollars for important projects.

Our faith conversation was eye-opening for me. She talked about studying the Dalai Lama and making her way through the mountains of Nepal. I will never forget her explanation of her faith. When asked, she said, "I am a Buddhist Christian." I loved this thought. It gave me more confidence about all kinds of thinking relative to my own developing faith. She said it with such confidence, ease, and a fine wry sense of humor that it made me smile. It was a moment of growth for me. There are so many ways people can bring faith into their lives. It is so individual. God knows we all have our own journeys. We must respect all forms of faith and carry on with love and understanding.

Two of my assistants joined the staff at an interesting time. My faith had grown as I was regularly attending church and feeling confident in my family, and team shares.

Wanisha Smith and Keturah Jackson were former Duke players who had impacted their teams greatly. Wanisha had a great career, and had to put up with a new coach for her senior year. I had arrived, and "Nish" Smith was the lone senior who had to adjust to many new things brought to Duke by me and the new staff.

Keturah has been an amazingly balanced and faithful person. The maturity of her faith traces back to her solid Christian upbringing in South Carolina. Her career was marked by leading her team, as a senior, to three points away from a Final Four. We battled so hard in that game. Just one play here or one call there proved to be the difference as we had to deal with that distressing defeat together.

One of my most powerful memories with both Nish and Keturah came off the court. I had decided to mark my newfound faith with a tattoo of John 14:27 on my right wrist. This thought came to me through three years of morning devotionals, and a love for the book of John. Of course, my husband's name is John, and that certainly made me feel more secure about my choice. That verse had come up repeatedly through my morning time. I just could not get away from it, because it reflected so much in my life. I asked Nish and Keturah, two women of faith with quite different faith journeys, to help me set up an appointment to get that tattoo. They smiled and laughed, and agreed immediately. I was nervous, but felt very supported. There certainly was no backing down. In the tattoo studio, as I lay on the table to begin the process, I squeezed the blood right out of Nish's hand as she held it. I did my old Lamaze breathing right through all that stinging. *Ouch!*

My melanoma memories came to mind as the hot stinging reminded me of the shots I received repeatedly to ensure that my malignant cells were removed. It did not take too long. I was proud and sure of my decision. I felt at peace and grateful to Nish and Keturah for the incredible support. My first tattoo at age fifty-three was a bit odd, but I believe that one should be over fifty to get a tattoo to really find out what matters in life. Most likely half your life is over, and there are so many experiences and stories that can fortify you for such a decision. Of course, I am not judging others and their choices. It is my sense of humor, and thought of the surreal nature of my life changes, that makes me remark on such a new choice for me. Over fifty, and just getting past some fears and doubts in my mind—and my first tattoo:

"Peace I leave with you; My peace I give to you; not as the world gives do I give to you. Do not let your heart be troubled, nor let it be afraid."
John 14:27

Sometimes in life a special person from long ago can reach out at the most perfect time. I coached Ruthie as a graduate assistant during my Auburn rookie days of learning and coaching. Ruthie was extraordinary. She was one of twenty children in a very devoted Christian family in McClain, Mississippi. I loved learning from her and coaching her with my raw passion, as I began to understand a great deal about running a championship basketball program at Auburn.

Many years later, after I decided to step away from Duke, I received a number of very thoughtful calls and texts. Ruthie gave me a call to say hello and check on things, and to discuss who might be the new head coach for Duke. We began to exchange stories of faith and adventure in all the great things Ruthie was doing relative to motivational talks and good works around the country. They do not call her "Mighty Ruthie" for nothing: she has an incredible physique, but her mental resilience is most impressive. She walks the word in every way, every day. She shared more about her life and how she had worked through adversity. She mentioned, out of the blue, that the scripture John 14:27 had been very dear in her own life. Ruthie and I had never had a faith conversation before. She had never called me to check up on me after our lives had gone in very different and busy directions. So after all that time, naturally, we both paused when we shared this clear God wink.

Ruthie talked with me about the time she went to speak on a Native American reservation. On that occasion, the woman who picked her up at the airport was very complimentary, and reminded Ruthie that her life seemed much like the book of Esther. She claimed that the words of *Esther 4:14* were perfect for Ruthie. With my mouth agape, and Ruthie still having a faithful deep pause relative to the first Scripture grace note, we treasured the moment of the second. Ruthie screamed into the phone. We both screamed of joy and irony together. It was if time had never passed. Ruthie and I, with many years elapsed since our coaching and her playing experiences including numerous Final Fours, had just shared our dearest verses within our personal faith world. Then, before we could really pull it together, I told Ruthie that I had an appointment that very week to get my second and final tattoo. I asked her if she could guess what is was—yes, indeed: Esther 4:14! Huge pause. A "wow" followed, as well.

Here was grace shared by two people far distant, in years and miles, as Ruthie lives in California now. A faithful connection occurred after thirty years of our knowing each other. I so appreciated Ruthie's call during a very new and challenging transitional time in my life. I could never have anticipated the conversation we would share.

"For if you remain silent at this time, relief and deliverance will arise for the Jews from another place and you and your father's house will perish. And who knows whether you have not attained royalty for such a time as this?"
Esther 4:14

Interesting stories arise in different ways. I have always loved connecting the dots with my players relative to events and coincidences in life. Prior to my faithful journey, I called those same thoughts, of time and place, exactly that: coincidences. But as my life has unfolded, there has been so much more to the stories while I was grounded in faith and God winks.

July 14, 2020 was special for me for a few reasons. I decided to get that second tattoo on that day. It was my parents' fifty-eighth wedding anniversary, and I was working hard on finishing my faith chapter of this book. I deemed myself ready to have the word on both of my inside wrists. Not too big, but just my way of committing to faith in my life with great interest in the faith work in others' lives as well.

My appointment was at one on a Tuesday afternoon. The artist was running late, but I patiently waited to relive that awful stinging sensation that was truly well worth it. I thought back to how a dear friend had mentioned the Book of Esther to suit me, and how I had a wonderful discussion with Joanie back in the fall. She had relayed the whole story to me as we took a drive on a recruiting trip in rural Michigan. Esther had come into my life without notice by way of a casual conversation, then had been fortified by one of my SICs, and I had chosen the verse that best represented this time in my life. This day was already a great day.

The artist began to work on me at approximately one-thirty. Of course, my phones were turned to silent as I worked with her to find the right font and size that best connected for me on my left inner wrist. That Lamaze breathing proved helpful again. I was beginning to figure out that the inner and lower part of the wrists are quite sensitive.

Afterward, as I returned to my car, I took a moment to think about my parents on this day, and how the significance of the timing gave me a chance to thank them for all they had done in my life. It also gave a great opportunity of forgiveness for any issues we had shared along the way. Families are beautifully imperfect. We all have family issues, some more than others. How can we get past those issues? We can remind ourselves of our journey, and work to forgive. Sometimes we can not forget, but the forgiveness frees us to move forward with peace. This is not easy, of course; forgiving can take years. But faith has that way of directing us to move forward and be free of all pain and judgments that come along the way.

After that prayer and thought, I glanced at my phone. It turned out that the pastor from my church, Pastor Clay, had called me at exactly the very time I was burning my faith Scripture onto my body in that tattoo parlor. I had not been to church since the Coronavirus outbreak. Pastor Clay had reached out a few times during my past three years as a rookie member of the church. As I was transitioning to a new life after leaving Duke, his timing was impeccable, and his words were even stronger and aligned with the meaning of the day.

Clay had called to say that he was checking on me. He had been asking God to give me a sense of excitement, and vision, for the next season of my life. He, a very busy man, was taking time to reach out to say he hoped things were going well for me and my family. There was excitement and vision, without a doubt. Just like Esther 4:14, newly present on my wrist, he had captured the moment in the timeliest fashion, to reach out support to me exactly as it all happened. Grace, indeed.

———————

There have been many other dear friends and coaches and players who have reached out to me in faith over the years. One of the most special is my dear friend Felisha Legette-Jack, my Virgo buddy, and a very good coach and person. Felisha is one of a kind, while faithfully leading her Buffalo team to its first ever Sweet Sixteen, and pushing Connecticut to their limits with a chance to compete in the Elite Eight. She is an amazingly talented coach, filled with passion for her team, and is unapologetic for spreading faith in their lives. Felisha served as a terrific assistant with me during my early years at Michigan State. She was always there, through the great times and those that were unfathomable, as well.

I, like many, will never forget the morning of September 11, 2001. I was head coach at Michigan State at the time. The trauma of such horrific events was nationwide. We collected the team immediately to talk, listen, and cope with such an unprecedented event in our country's history. The shocking news sent fear and uncertainty through every American. Our team was scared, and at first there were few details to share. We all joined hands to pray. Felisha was normally our leader of Faith and the prayer giver. Just before she got started, I felt a need—a strong urge—to lead this group in prayer as the head coach. Of course, I had never led a group prayer before in my life. Some might say I was moved by the spirit. I was indeed moved, and lifted in confidence, to assert these words of faith. Praying before knowing is a memory of faith I will never forget.

"Lord, please give us the strength and courage and hope during this most challenging time. May good conquer evil and may we all rise together as one nation and people during this horrific time. Amen."

———————————

Ellen Geraghty is another former player who captivated and shared faith with me well after I coached her at the University of Maine, and she is yet another SIC to surface at exactly the right time. Although I served as her coach years ago, we began our faith conversations when I was coaching at Duke and truly beginning to understand more about our personal journeys of faith. A relationship between player and coach can keep developing many years after time on the court. Ellen and I have continued to learn more about each other, and move closer, ever since we both began to understand how God's grace has truly impacted our lives. The special connection with so many people regarding faith has been one of the greatest experiences of my life, right alongside finding John, and giving birth to two great kids. Can I get an "amen"?

POSTGAME

Stepping away from Duke was one of the most difficult transitions in my life. How do you "call it" after doing something for so many years where your schedule is dictated to you, and the directives and goals are so very clear to all on a daily basis? How do you walk away from a passion for coaching, and a daily lifestyle, that has driven you for so long? How do you walk away from amazing women and some unfinished dreams at a special place, after working with so many great people for thirteen years? How do you reconcile wondering if you will coach again after a twenty-eight-year career filled with memories? For me, such questions abound with uncertainty and trepidation for the future.

Of course, there is no easy answer to this feeling of significant change. My thoughts return to the simpler things that have meant the most over the years, including the practices, the training table meals shared with special people like Sam Lingle, the travel, the overall day-to-day camaraderie with the team and staff. There is a sense of wins and losses, and championships won or lost, but those memories are not the prevailing thoughts. As a coach who has always loved sports camp, I find myself thinking of those bright-eyed and eager campers who look up to the players and coaches as if we can move mountains. Hilarious question-and-answer segments with the players were always a true highlight.

Most noticeable about coaching as a profession is the wonderful change of seasons, year by year, month by month and week by week. The composite four-year opportunity to impact young lives, and influence thinking and growth, is no doubt the reason the profession is so demanding, but so interesting as well. For me, there is a new sense of reluctance as I step away into another space of influence and growth. A hesitation, a pause, and a deep sigh find their way into each new day for me, as the *former* coach, a label I am still not completely comfortable with. And there is uncertainty over what's in store in the years to come. I still wonder if my decision to step away from coaching at age fifty-five came prematurely.

Without a doubt, I miss the people and the relationships. Many of those who I knew in coaching have continued with their journeys and responsibilities. Staffs have changed, the players have moved on, and the program I ran continues seamlessly. I quickly realized, upon departure, we are all *replaceable* in life. The players, the team now has another coach. The gap between what was, and what now is, grows daily. Things grow eerily quiet. For some time, it is as if I have less to say and offer. The inner quiet is matched with a more contemplative exterior personality. This is not a permanent state of mind completely, but it is a transitional state of mind that seems unavoidable, and lingers at least for a while.

Transitional times, and those that bring uncertainty, are generally the hardest times for us all. Our country, and world today, is coping with such issues. It's hard to fathom all the other family and work transitions that are occurring at the same time. Such times call for an even more important awareness for *how* we think. The conversations we choose to have with ourselves might just be our most important conversations of the day.

Strong words and thoughts from mentors become clear and impactful. The concept of *self-talk* is overused a bit, but very applicable and helpful when confronting change. As I entered some of the most challenging transitions of my life, I found myself striving to come back to the simple concept of *gratitude* for the experiences

I had. Given the challenges we all go through, this simple attitude check is not so easy as levels of uncertainty continue to fluctuate almost daily. We are tortured by the unknowns, and want answers and consistency.

Years ago, in my senior statement in the Brunswick High School yearbook I said, "The secret of success is constancy to purpose." – Benjamin Disraeli. I remember thinking how profound that quote sounded, but how simple it really seemed as I thought about how it applied to life. Of course, I did not want to be known just as a "jock" at school. I appreciated the erudite nature of the quote as it was printed under my senior photo in the Brunswick High School Yearbook of 1983. I marvel at how its application has been so critical and spot-on. Finding a daily purpose appears to be the key to the ability to move through these moments—for me personally, and for the precarious times worldwide.

Finding that purpose amidst uncertainty of the future takes some real soul searching. It is hard to talk about situational relativism of uncertainty when your life is being altered at such a steady daily pace. All of our situations count equally for what they are, and how they bring fear and joy into our lives. Stepping away means much more than just a potential pause of coaching and a change of career. It is more a state of mind, impacted by many factors, large and small. After twenty-eight years of being a head coach, my own journey to start anew is adrift with many transitions occurring simultaneously. Purpose remains the key to fighting through the emotions, and changes, of these personal transitional times. I hope I can stay in this place of good thinking. I need to remember that each day provides a new challenge. Truly, some days are much better than others in my search for purpose.

Scheduling my days with any productive activity, or even rest time, appears to be half the battle in moving through these life pauses. I sometimes think of my former colleagues who are still in the game, and wonder how they are navigating the uncertain and confusing nature of coaching. At this writing in the fall of 2020, the Coronavirus has disrupted the day-to-day constancy we all crave. These times are so unprecedented, and they can paralyze actions and thinking.

The rancor over whether to play football, basketball and all sports seasons amid the pandemic exposes the financial demands of each university in supporting their athletic departments. So many dramatic changes appear imminent, and unwelcome, relative to the potential cutbacks and other effects on our higher institutions of learning.

When one is moved to make dramatic change, the reality is that it generally has a macro motivation. The singular motive does not exist. As a mountaineer, you climb and climb, step by step, without ever truly knowing what you will see as you approach the summit to get a clear view. Often, the view on the other side is not clear, but cloudy and confusing in its presentation. These days, I feel like a mountaineer eager to see the other side, but wondering if it can be as beautiful as I hope.

There are some clear principles that have been circulating in my mind, nuggets of wisdom that I gleaned over the years to help prepare me for the other side of the summit. I remind myself that as a former coach I no longer have to perform to be accepted. In fact, there is an element of performance in most any career choice. We are often measured by results. In coaching, it is very clear what is a good performance, and what is something less. Our feedback is direct. Fans have a clear role in evaluating performances. Usually though, the best judges are the coaches and players themselves.

I have learned that we do not have to have good circumstances to be grateful. We often talk about, rely on, or try to change our circumstances to maximize outcomes. But can we stay in that place of gratitude for the simplest things? Daily gratitude is the trick. We all fall victim to missing the big picture, and losing those little bits, those small things that end up being the big things.

After having left Duke and examining my own life, I have

resolved that I do not have to control everything before I am at peace. This was a tough realization for someone who, as a coach, was in charge and in control. Now, I look at peace as a state of mind to be pursued daily, the ultimate destination. It's not necessary to get that new home, a new place, a new job, a new something, a new season, to achieve that peace of mind.

There is no doubt that all coaches must have some control, and thrive on preparing for all circumstances. For me, now, the circumstances are unprecedented worldwide. Control is impossible to maintain as it presupposes proactive action by all. These times are full of reactive measures filled with conjecture and innuendo. We all are navigating the most challenging opponent of our times. Team thinking and connection is what we need if we are to battle through all the current and future challenges.

———————

Sports and coaching can be a great metaphor for so many things. One of the greater concepts of coaching and teaching and players competing is that we truly never arrive at that peaceful, contented place. There is no endpoint. Life experiences and demands keep rolling on day-to-day, season-to-season. Expectations never fade. I am reminded of a conversation with an old friend. She assisted a team to a national championship. The team found a way to be the best and win it all. Then, one of the players made a late-night call to their coach with a most profound question:

"What now? What do I do now?"

Truly, that feeling of being at the top of the mountain, with the incredible view, but filled with clouds and wonderment, can be unsteady and overwhelming at the same time. Pondering what's next is a difficult way of dealing with achievement. We all strive to get to places and achieve goals and dreams. But, the "what now" question reminds us of how we need to think and work on ourselves to accept the continuum of life, and how the process of achievement never quite stops. This can be exhausting on the surface. But, finding joy has much to do with how we handle the day-to-day tasks, even knowing that many events are outside our control, and we do not always know the why and the what now. Reason and faith can drive us forward to an even better space.

As we move forward, we make a choice on how to think and process our transitions and life changes. Here are three more thoughts that can quiet the emotional angst and anxiety spurred by transition: *What do I control? What do I influence? What can't I influence in my life?* Sorting through these additional three points of thinking has helped me keep on task with my own transition. We control so much of our day. We choose whether to make our bed, whether to eat right, whether to go to work, whether to exercise, and so on. The choices are never-ending in our day-to-day life.

Influence is a critical piece to relationships and productivity. For a coach, influence is our currency. We influence to win, to make positive changes. Coaches, especially at the amateur level, are in the business of developing people. I can influence my family and friends. But, as a mentor and basically a life coach, can I influence others to make a difference in their own lives? Can I be a broader coach, and go beyond the court and affect lives within mental health and sport for the long term? These can be terrifying questions for someone who truly has been in the business of influencing young minds, especially the minds of elite athletes. I can only succeed in this process by repeating to myself the third reminder—what I cannot influence in my life: pandemics, weather, actions of others, health, choices of others, and perceptions and some personal circumstances. We all should use these reminders as guides for how we cope and move forward with change. I have tried to do so in the wake of stepping away from Duke, which was clearly one of the biggest changes of my professional and personal life.

As time passed, the phones have become quieter. The reality of a new life has set in slowly. The initial outpouring of texts and calls upon my leaving Duke was overwhelming and greatly appreciated. But, after all the care, I have become a civilian in a sense.

I am no longer in the public eye, but I still think often about a new direction in life that would build on my past. I love that people still refer to me as Coach P. That name is a reminder of all the special coaching times earned through a lot of years, and countless hours spent in the gym. I am still not eager to retire that name because it remains who I am and is still an accurate description of who I will become, perhaps on the sidelines once again directing a team, or coaching someone struggling with a personal or mental health issue.

I was advised to wait to write this book until after I retired from coaching in the belief that no one would hire me after I revealed my story. This was advice from a well-meaning person, and is evidence that we have not come far enough to accept and acknowledge mental illness as a manageable disease for many.

Sharing a life experience does not render a person an expert in the field of mental health advocacy. But it does speak a path that can be carved out of something frightening and shocking, something that as a nation we have faced together, a reality that has strained our collective mental resolve.

———————

As I was writing this book in the spring of 2020, the unthinkable and unimaginable happened to all of us when the coronavirus expanded to a full worldwide pandemic—it slowed time and brought about many new terms that we will never forget: "Shelter in place;" "Social distancing;" "Covid-19;" "flattened the curve;" and the parade of masks, where smiles are hidden, for everyone in any public spaces.

Sports seasons were cancelled; families have lost homes; schools are closed and classes taken remotely. Loved ones are getting sick and dying by the tens of thousands. There is much political hostility. Riots. Suicides and depression on the rise. Isolation.

This tragic chapter in our lives serves as a reminder of the fragility of our current and future mental health of our country and around the world. Awareness, education, and storytelling are among the keys to providing a dialogue that leads to coping and healing. Exercise, nutrition, alcohol in moderation are also part of a formula for mental stability.

Never before has there been more need to discuss mental health as an actionable affliction. I hope that my story somehow contributes to a more robust, open and honest dialogue about taking care of our minds.

As a nation, we need to have a clear path to help the affected, just as we would for any other ailment or disease. The forming of a team, where all parts connect and generate energy and execution for each other, is critical. How do we coordinate the doctors, therapists, and potential mentors who have gone through a similar experience? How can we smooth the recovery plan just as when fighting any disease? Of course, we're already working hard on these components of a solution, but we can become better and more fluid in our approach.

———————————

I want to end this book on another uplifting note as it pertains to my chosen profession. I am hopeful for some of the possible positive unintended consequences of the horrific and scary time that our entire world and nation have been going through as of this writing. The decisions to play sports during the pandemic have been very controversial. Teams have to compete with few or no fans. The love of the game and the competition by itself, without the adoration and cheers from supporters, makes the competitors dig deep and really compete from the heart alone and through their teammates.

Without the in-person limelight of filled arenas and stadiums, and the constant adoration of fans, who are we, as athletes?

There is an old coach saying that, "It is what you do when no one is looking" that marks you as a special player. Never has that been more relevant.

Despite some TV coverage, athletes are being reminded why they got into sport: that they're playing for the pure love of game. It gives all pause to see all sports differently, to appreciate the game and not just the celebrity, to depend on each other ever more so than before. We are all reminded of the randomness of life.

Athletes no longer take for granted the value in representing their school or city. Coaches are even more protective and reassuring, enjoying their players and sport without the usual scrutiny and expectations. Coaching for the love of teaching has found new relevance. Coaches teach to survive the unknowns together.

Dealing with so much uncertainty and living with the outcomes in the microcosm of sport is helpful. The national champions of any sport may just be the teams that listen the most about the dangers of not social spacing, show discipline when faced with these ultimate challenges, and obviously have talent enough to play at the highest level. Randomness and uncertainty fill our worlds. But therein lies opportunity to reconnect with what is important in life and sport.

———————

At times, I observe people struggling to keep their balance. We learn to recognize the signs just with observation, and maybe a conversation or two. My empathy meter is at an all-time high, as I have learned to sort through the dynamics of family, and try to understand my own genetic code that can bring about mood disorders. I have learned to cope with a variety of childhood experiences that, in retrospect, make much more sense.

I always have taught that our own unique differences make us special. Coaching is seeing and teaching young people, or any age person, to see their future image of themselves. We never arrive. Life is a fluid and beautiful gift and challenge to us all. With even the most unfathomable scenarios, like what the world has experienced in 2020 and will experience beyond, we will find a way to survive and thrive. Much will be learned from all the lessons, sadness and successes, from the Coronavirus outbreak. We all have a chance to change and improve our own future image. We can be in a better place. Mental health can be seen through the right lens and will be understood at levels never possible before.

ACKNOWLEDGMENTS

Of course, there are so many people to thank. Thank you to all my teams and staffs that gave me strength and taught me more about life than I could ever imagine. To Kate, Bobby, Selena, Ashleigh and Cat, your loyalty has been so very special. A heartfelt thank you to my coaching staff in my last year, Keturah Jackson, Wanisha Smith, Sam Miller, and Jim Corrigan who had to endure my departure without the appropriate support. You four will always be remembered as incredible Warriors for life, and we were just getting started! A unique and very special thank you to the UMaine women who supported me and my family during incredibly challenging times. Your loyalty and leadership went far beyond your years and will never be forgotten. My family and I are so very grateful for the life in coaching we were able to continue because of your courage and willingness to seek truth and rise above the challenges of the day.

To the Michigan State Spartans, thank you for buying into Coach P life and philosophy so we could charge to the top of the mountain in five fabulous years. To all the Duke women, thank you for an incredible thirteen-year run as we strived to achieve the highest level together. Your Duke pride and passion was a joy to work with every single day. A special thank you to all the wonderful athletic directors that gave me and my family opportunities of a lifetime, Mike Ploszek, Dr. Suzanne Tyler, Dr. Clarence Underwood, the late Ron Mason, Joe

Alleva, and Dr. Kevin White. Thank you to the great men's college coaches who I had the privilege to serve with for twenty-eight years, Rudy Keeling, John Giannini, Tom Izzo and Mike Krzyzewski. A heartfelt thank you to Nike for the incredible relationships built over the past twenty-seven years. Another very special thank you to Joe Ciampi for believing a Maine person could thrive and succeed in the deep South of Auburn, AL! Your belief in me as a coach while learning from you, changed the path of my life in the best ways. A big shout out to all the Auburn Lady Tigers and staffs that welcomed a rookie coach from Maine into one of the greatest programs of all time.

Thank you to my dear friends from Maine to Michigan to North Carolina and nationwide who have supported me and my family and known us very personally for a long time. There are so many great people and fans to thank as a result of our special three-school journey. A special thank you to my two former MSU assistants, Felisha Legette-Jack and Katie Abrahamson for their loyalty and dear friendship while providing such great leadership to the University of Buffalo and University of Central Florida respectively.

Thank you to my incredible personal "team" of doctors and support people who have been the amazing women leaders in my life. You all have taught me so much about balance, the brain and full living while managing a mood disorder. To all my student-athletes and parents, thank you for reading this book. I trust you still feel, and know, that I gave my heart and soul to each and everyone of you.

A very special thank you to my wonderful sister-in-law, Eleanor McCallie Cooper, a successful author and dear family member, who has been with me every step of the way with this project. And to my son Jack Wyatt, for making the writing of this book possible with his countless tutorials on how to use and write with a computer, after I spent so many years of having others cover up for my poor computer skills.

Thank you, Holly Barnett, for starting and cultivating Team Secret Warrior, and for your sound advice always. Thank you to my

Duke former player Faith Suggs, special daughter Maddie McCallie, and dear niece Sarah Clement for sharing their thoughts as very strong women from a special generation. for rounding a Team Secret Warrior. Thank you to Eleanor Hoover for being a part of Team Secret Warrior and for your wisdom and consulting while bringing Malbert Smith to our team. Thank you Malbert Smith for your tremendous support, leadership, expertise, and love for the entrepreneurial spirit in us all. Thank you to Barb St. Clair for your friendship and those infamous Croasdaile Crazies. Thank you to all the people, families and players who were comfortable in sharing their names and stories for this writing. Thank you to my dear high school coach and his wife, Fred and Kathy Koerber, and to the late Allen Graffam, for great support and teaching me how to shoot a basketball and truly love the game. Thank you to Dr. Lonny Rosen for your countless hours of mentorship and friendship. A special thank you to Nancy Roderick for being there for all times, good and bad. Thank you, Terry Burke and Stan Bagley, for our amazing long-term friendship and shared understanding of mood disorders. A special and very dear thank you to Sarah Palisi Chapin for bringing insights, experience, and expanding the audience of *Secret Warrior*, while bringing such energy and joy to this project. A huge and grateful thank you to Joe Coccaro and Marshall McClure, two incredibly gifted editors with a great deal of patience in sorting through the words, ideas and stories behind this book. A thank you to Skyler Kratofil, a gifted designer. Thank you to the special team behind the journey led by Sharon Delaney McCloud and Amina Fisher. Profuse thank you to Melanie Sanders for your creativity and commitment to telling the story with great dignity and grace. Thank you Jason Tyson for your strategic mind and incredible care for this story to be shared worldwide! And, of course, thank you to John Koehler for believing in this book, and for his timely sense of humor and great faith in a coach turned full-time author who needed and welcomed much literary coaching along the way.

To my mother and father, thank you for your incredible support and love throughout my career and life. To my Maine family, Rich, my supportive and fun-loving brother, and Carolyn, my super sis in every way, and to Brian, an incredible brother-in-law, a profuse and loving thank you to you all. To my beautiful nieces, Meg, Allie, Sarah, Camille and Catie: keep doing your thing! We adore all of you.

And, of course, a continuous and ongoing thank you to my dear husband of twenty-nine years, John. Your unwavering support, and science-driven mind of reason over emotion, combined with incredible patience, has led this family through our challenging and best times. You are one of the great warriors in our lives. To all the Warriors out there who can celebrate our "secrets" with dignity, education, courage and grace in every circumstance, we all say thank you as you navigate your "best self" while being "good to you," and patient with the process of brain health.

As I said to Faith, there is a time to share our stories. I strive to remain Coach P with a long awaited hope of helping others and for all to find their balance while living their unique selves and trusting in all possibilities. Dwelling in possibility is so worth it, and the only way to truly be free.

CPSIA information can be obtained
at www.ICGtesting.com
Printed in the USA
BVHW071015180221
600496BV00002B/139